Communications in Computer and Information Science 1017

Commenced Publication in 2007
Founding and Former Series Editors:
Phoebe Chen, Alfredo Cuzzocrea, Xiaoyong Du, Orhun Kara, Ting Liu,
Krishna M. Sivalingam, Dominik Ślęzak, Takashi Washio, and Xiaokang Yang

Editorial Board Members

Simone Diniz Junqueira Barbosa
  Pontifical Catholic University of Rio de Janeiro (PUC-Rio),
  Rio de Janeiro, Brazil
Joaquim Filipe
  Polytechnic Institute of Setúbal, Setúbal, Portugal
Ashish Ghosh
  Indian Statistical Institute, Kolkata, India
Igor Kotenko
  St. Petersburg Institute for Informatics and Automation of the Russian
  Academy of Sciences, St. Petersburg, Russia
Junsong Yuan
  University at Buffalo, The State University of New York, Buffalo, NY, USA
Lizhu Zhou
  Tsinghua University, Beijing, China

More information about this series at http://www.springer.com/series/7899

Tristan Cazenave · Abdallah Saffidine ·
Nathan Sturtevant (Eds.)

Computer Games

7th Workshop, CGW 2018
Held in Conjunction with the 27th International Conference
on Artificial Intelligence, IJCAI 2018
Stockholm, Sweden, July 13, 2018
Revised Selected Papers

 Springer

Editors
Tristan Cazenave
LAMSADE, Université Paris-Dauphine
Paris, France

Abdallah Saffidine (iD)
University of New South Wales
Sydney, Australia

Nathan Sturtevant
University of Alberta
Edmonton, Canada

ISSN 1865-0929   ISSN 1865-0937 (electronic)
Communications in Computer and Information Science
ISBN 978-3-030-24336-4   ISBN 978-3-030-24337-1   (eBook)
https://doi.org/10.1007/978-3-030-24337-1

This Springer imprint is published by the registered company Springer Nature Switzerland AG
The registered company address is: Gewerbestrasse 11, 6330 Cham, Switzerland

Preface

These proceedings contain the papers of the Computer Games Workshop (CGW 2018) held in Stockholm, Sweden. The workshop took place on July 13, 2018, in conjunction with the 27th International Conference on Artificial Intelligence (IJCAI 2018). The Computer and Games Workshop series is an international forum for researchers interested in all aspects of artificial intelligence (AI) and computer game playing. Earlier workshops took place in Montpellier, France (2012), Beijing, China (2013), Prague, Czech Republic (2014), Buenos Aires, Argentina (2015), New York, USA (2016), and Melbourne, Australia (2017).

For the seventh edition of the Computer Games Workshop, 15 papers were submitted in 2018. Each paper was sent to three reviewers. In the end, ten contributions were accepted for presentation at the workshop, of which eight made it into these proceedings.

The workshop also featured an invited talk by Marlos C. Machado titled "Revisiting the Arcade Learning Environment: Evaluation Protocols and Open Problems for General Agents," joint work with Marc G. Bellemare, Erik Talvitie, Joel Veness, Matthew Hausknecht, Michael Bowling.

The published papers cover a wide range of topics related to computer games. They collectively discuss abstract games such as the game of Go (two papers) and video games. Three papers deal with video games, two papers on General Game Playing, and one discusses a Web-based game. Here we provide a brief outline of the eight contributed papers.

"Spatial Average Pooling for Computer Go," is by Tristan Cazenave. The paper addresses Deep Reinforcement Learning for computer Go. It shows that using spatial average pooling improves a value network for computer Go.

"Iterative Tree Search in General Game Playing with Incomplete Information," is authored by Armin Chitizadeh, and Michael Thielscher. In General Game Playing (GGP) with incomplete information the lifted HyperPlay technique, which is based on model sampling, is the state of the art. However, this method is known not to model opponents properly, with the effect that it generates only pure strategies and is short-sighted when valuing information. The papers addresses this limitations using fictitious play to introduce an iterative tree search algorithm for incomplete-information GGP.

"TextWorld: A Learning Environment for Text-Based Games," is written by Marc-Alexandre Côté, Ákos Kádár, Xingdi Yuan, Ben Kybartas, Tavian Barnes, Emery Fine, James Moore, Matthew Hausknecht, Layla El Asri, Mahmoud Adada, Wendy Tay, and Adam Trischler. The paper introduces TextWorld, a sandbox learning environment for the training and evaluation of reinforcement learning agents on text-based games. TextWorld is a Python library that handles interactive play-through of text games. It enables one to cast text-based games in the reinforcement learning formalism and to develop a set of benchmark games, and evaluate several baseline agents on this set.

"What's in A Game? The Effect of Game Complexity on Deep Reinforcement Learning," is authored by Erdem Emekligil, Ethem Alpaydın. Deep Reinforcement Learning works on some games better than others. The paper proposes to evaluate the complexity of each game using a number of factors (the size of the search space, existence/absence of enemies, existence/absence of intermediate reward, and so on). Experiments are conducted on simplified Maze and Pacman environments.

"Analyzing the Impact of Knowledge and Search in Monte Carlo Tree Search in Go," is written by Farhad Haqiqat and Martin Müller. The paper focuses on identifying the effects of different types of knowledge on the behavior of the Monte Carlo tree search algorithm, using the game of Go as a case study. Performance of each type of knowledge and of deeper search is measured according to the move prediction rate on games played by professional players and the playing strength of an implementation in the open source program Fuego.

"Statistical GGP Game Decomposition," is authored by Aline Hufschmitt, Jean-Noël Vittaut, and Nicolas Jouandeau. The paper presents a statistical approach for the decomposition of games in the GGP framework. General game players can drastically decrease game search cost if they hold a decomposed version of the game. Previous works on decomposition rely on syntactical structures, which can be missing from the game description, or on the disjunctive normal form of the rules, which is very costly to compute. The program has been tested on 597 games. Given a timeout of 1 hour and few playouts (1k), their method successfully provides an expert-like decomposition for 521 of them.

"Towards Embodied StarCraft II Winner Prediction," is by Vanessa Volz, Mike Preuss, and Mathias Kirk Bonde. Realtime strategy games (and especially StarCraft II) are currently becoming the "next big thing" in game AI, as building human competitive bots for complex games is still not possible. However, the abundance of existing game data makes StarCraft II an ideal testbed for machine learning. The paper attempts to use this for establishing winner predictors. Such predictors can be made available to human players as a supportive AI component, but they can more importantly be used as state evaluations in order to inform strategic planning for a bot.

"MOBA-Slice: A Time Slice-Based Evaluation Framework of Relative Advantage Between Teams in MOBA Games," is written by Lijun Yu, Dawei Zhang, Xiangqun Chen, Xing Xie. Multiplayer online battle arena (MOBA) is currently one of the most popular genres of digital games around the world. It is hard for humans and algorithms to evaluate the real-time game situation or predict the game result. The paper introduces MOBA-Slice, a time slice-based evaluation framework of relative advantage between teams in MOBA games. MOBA-Slice is a quantitative evaluation method based on learning, similar to the value network of AlphaGo. MOBA-Slice is applied to Defense of the Ancients 2 (DotA2), a typical and popular MOBA game. Experiments on a large number of match replays show that the model works well on arbitrary matches.

These proceedings would not have been produced without the help of many persons. In particular, we would like to mention the authors and reviewers for their help. Moreover, the organizers of IJCAI 2018 contributed substantially by bringing the researchers together.

March 2018

Tristan Cazenave
Abdallah Saffidine
Nathan Sturtevant

Organization

Program Chairs

Tristan Cazenave   Université Paris-Dauphine, France
Abdallah Saffidine   University of New South Wales, Australia
Nathan Sturtevant   University of Denver, USA

Program Committee

Hendrik Baier   University of York, UK
Édouard Bonnet   École Normale Supérieure de Lyon, France
Bruno Bouzy   University of Paris Descartes, France
Michael Buro   University of Alberta, Canada
Amy K. Hoover   New Jersey Institute of Technology, USA
Nicolas Jouandeau   University of Paris 8, France
Levi Lelis   Universidade Federal de Viçosa, Brazil
Jialin Liu   Queen Mary University of London, UK
Henryk Michalewski   University of Warsaw, Poland
Martin Müller   University of Alberta, Canada
Santiago Ontañón   Drexel University, USA
Joseph C. Osborn   University California Santa Cruz, USA
Aske Plaat   Leiden University, The Netherlands
Malcolm Ryan   Macquarie University, Australia
Jean-Noël Vittaut   University of Paris 8, France

Contents

Video Games

Towards Embodied StarCraft II Winner Prediction

Vanessa Volz[1](✉), Mike Preuss[2], and Mathias Kirk Bonde[3]

[1] TU Dortmund University, Dortmund, Germany
vanessa.volz@tu-dortmund.de
[2] Westfälische Wilhelms-Universität Münster, Münster, Germany
[3] University of Copenhagen, Copenhagen, Denmark

Abstract. Realtime strategy games (and especially StarCraft II) are currently becoming the 'next big thing' in Game AI, as building human competitive bots for complex games is still not possible. However, the abundance of existing game data makes StarCraft II an ideal testbed for machine learning. We attempt to use this for establishing winner predictors that in strong contrast to existing methods rely on partial information available to one player only. Such predictors can be made available to human players as a supportive AI component, but they can more importantly be used as state evaluations in order to inform strategic planning for a bot. We show that it is actually possible to reach accuracies near to the ones reported for full information with relatively simple techniques. Next to performance, we also look at the interpretability of the models that may be valuable for supporting human players as well as bot creators.

Keywords: StarCraft II · Outcome prediction · Interpretability · Embodied gamestate evaluation

1 Introduction

Being able to evaluate a game state in terms of imbalance towards (advantage for) one player is crucial to many types of generally applicable game-playing algorithms, such as Monte-Carlo tree search (MCTS) [7]. Heuristics based on expert knowledge are often used as an evaluation function (see survey in [20]), but depending on the game in question, such a measure is difficult to construct and verify. It is therefore beneficial to be able to learn game characteristics from replay data instead, as this approach avoids human bias and is also generalisable to other games, an important topic in current research [14]. One possible binary (component of an) evaluation function of a given game state is whether the player is likely to win or to lose. In this paper, we thus investigate embodied winner prediction, i.e. only using information available to a single player (or bot).

© Springer Nature Switzerland AG 2019
T. Cazenave et al. (Eds.): CGW 2018, CCIS 1017, pp. 3–22, 2019.
https://doi.org/10.1007/978-3-030-24337-1_1

In fact, such information may also be helpful to players because the data driven heuristic may be more accurate than their own estimation of the current state of the game, or be accurate in cases that are difficult to decide for a human. We will address the differences between the (expert) human and machine learned judgment of the overall game state.

Being able to predict the winner of a game is also important in the context of dynamic difficulty adaptation [11] and in context of AI-assisted game design, e.g. when evaluating the decidedness or tension of a game [6]. Furthermore, the construction of such a predictor can improve the understanding of a game's characteristics and act as a basis for developing new strategies for human and AI players. The characteristics could even be tracked over time in order to obtain knowledge about the meta of the game.

The identification of game characteristics is especially important since AIs in commercial games typically rely on domain knowledge, because more general approaches would not fulfill resource or believability constraints.[1]. To do that, the predictor should be interpretable as well. This has the added benefit of facilitating the detection of overfitting issues.

In this paper, we thus investigate the feasibility of constructing a model for winner prediction for a complex AAA game that is both (1) embodied and (2) interpretable. To this end, we test different strategies, such as incorporating data from multiple ticks and vary feature sets and models. We choose to conduct our study on StarCraft II, as related AIs are a topic of active research [21] and we can assume that winner prediction is a challenging task. Additionally, as of recently, suitable data is available [22] in high quantity. The fact that the subject of winner prediction in StarCraft (II) has been approached previously (cf. related work Sect. 2.2) also demonstrates a high interest. However, to our knowledge, there are no winner prediction methods that do not assume full observability of all features and at the same time are interpretable and tested on human vs. human replays (cf. Sect. 2.2). We aim to fill this gap with the work detailed in this paper. Due to the lack of a single consistent definition of interpretability, we instead anecdotally investigate it using the opinions and understanding of an expert StarCraft II player.

In the following section, we first briefly introduce the StarCraft series and then review the state-of-the-art of winner prediction on RTS games. Based on our literature overview, we formulate several hypotheses to test in this paper. To this end, we first describe our experimental setup in Sect. 3, including our data collection and preprocessing approach, as well as the prediction models we tested. We describe the results of our experiments and hypothesis tests in Sect. 4. Afterwards, we analyse the interpretability of the obtained models. We conclude our paper in Sect. 5 with a summary and possible directions of future work.

---

[1] Duygu Cakmak: *The grand strategy approach to AI* at Emotech Meet AI 9 (London), March 22nd 2018.

2   Background and Related Work

2.1   StarCraft Series

Game Description. StarCraft II[2] is a popular real-time strategy (RTS) game with a science-fiction theme released by Blizzard in 2010, which was followed up with further expansion packs in 2013, 2015, and 2016. It is the second game in the series, the first StarCraft game was published in 1998. StarCraft II was designed as an E-Sport [5] and has a massive following, regular tournaments (e.g. World Championship Series) and professional players.

StarCraft II features three playable races (Terran, Protoss, Zerg) and several game modes (1v1, 2v2, 3v3, 4v4 and campaign). Each player spawns with a town-hall building and a small number of workers at a predetermined location on a map, their base. The players can construct additional buildings, which can be used to produce more workers and military units. The properties of the available buildings and units are determined by the race played. There are additional upgrade mechanisms available to buildings as well as units. Buildings, units, and upgrades require different amounts of minerals and vespene gas, the two resources in the game. Both can be gathered by worker units. The supply value, which may be increased by additional buildings, poses a limit to the number of units that can be built by a player.

The player that successfully destroys all their opponent's buildings has won the game. The game also ends if a player concedes or if a stalemate is detected by the game.

StarCraft as Research Environment. The first game version, and specifically its expansion pack *StarCraft: Brood War*, have been used in research as a benchmark and competition framework[3] for AI agents since 2009 [21]. In 2017, DeepMind and Blizzard published the *StarCraft II Learning Environment (SC2LE)* [22]. The SC2LE provides an interface for AI agents to interact with a multi-platform version of StarCraft II and supports the analysis of previously recorded games.

Specifically, the SC2LE offers an interface through which a large set of game state observations[4] can be made available for every game tick in a replay or in real-time. The information that can be obtained includes raw data on features such as unit health and unit type in the form of heatmaps. At the same time, it also includes aggregated information that is usually displayed to game observers that can help to characterise a player's progress. Examples include the resource collection rate and the number of units destroyed represented as their value in resources. The SC2LE consists of multiple sub-projects, which include, among other things, a python wrapper library pysc2[5] used in this paper.

---

[2] https://starcraft2.com.
[3] http://bwapi.github.io/.
[4] https://github.com/deepmind/pysc2/blob/master/docs/environment.md.
[5] https://github.com/deepmind/pysc2.

Even before releasing SC2LE, Blizzard has been allowing players to save their own StarCraft II games to a file using the .S2Replay format. These replays can then be watched using the StarCraft II software and even analysed using the *S2 Protocol* published by Blizzard. s2protocol[6] is a Python library that provides a standalone tool to read information from .S2Replay files. The files contain repositories with different information. The metadata repository, for example, contains general information on the game and the players, such as the result, the selected races, the game map, and the duration of the game as well as technical details such as the StarCraft II build number. More details on the recorded features, their interpretation, and how they are used in this paper can be found in Sect. 3.

2.2 Outcome Prediction

With the release of SC2LE, the authors of the corresponding paper [22] also presented several use cases for their research environment, among them predicting the outcome of a game given a game state. They test three different neural networks to predict game outcome based only on the observations a player makes at a given time. The two best performing models both contain two convolutional networks with 2 layers and 16 and 32 filters, respectively. To represent the game state, they use spatial features gathered from the minimap, as well as other measures observable by the player, such as the supply cap. With this setup, they are able to reach a prediction accuracy of about 60% after 8 min of game time and approach 70% after 20 min.

However, due to the complexity of the models, as well as the applications of learned spatial features, it is very difficult to interpret the resulting networks. While not absolutely necessary, interpretability is a nice feature both for understanding game characteristics, as well as biasing AIs with the discovered patterns. More importantly, more complex models always are more prone to overfitting. In this paper we therefore investigate how better interpretable and smaller models perform in comparison.

Additionally, the authors of [22] recognise that training a predictor not only on information from the current gametick, but also including previous ticks in the input, would likely increase prediction accuracy. We investigate this hypothesis in this work by integrating different amounts of historic data as well as different aggregation methods.

Lastly, the input that is used in the paper heavily depends on the exploratory behaviour of the players. It is unclear how different scouting behaviours and the resulting difference in information might influence the predictor. We thus chose to focus on directly interpretable measures that are not influenced by information gathering methods. However, it would be interesting to investigate this further and compare it to predictors trained on fully observable game states. In this case, we decided to investigate the baseline, i.e. no opponent information, instead.

---

[6] https://github.com/Blizzard/s2protocol.

Besides the paper described above, there are a number of related publications on outcome predictors for StarCraft: Brood War, some of which are also used within AI agents. In [15], for example, the authors predict the winner of StarCraft matches using several time-dependent and -independent features collected from human vs. human replays from the dataset described in [16]. The authors of [15] stress the fact that, in contrast to many other publications (such as [17, 18]), they work on data that was not artificially generated or collected from simplified StarCraft versions. Additionally, while similar work had previously only considered Protoss vs. Protoss match-ups using the same dataset [8], in [15] the authors investigate how separate models for each race match-up can be combined. Both publications use features that express the difference between the two players at a given time, e.g. in terms of number of units, as well as a measure based on random rollouts similar to LDT2 (life time damage a unit can inflict) as proposed in [10]. In [8], the authors reach an average prediction accuracy of 58.72% for 5–10 min of observed gameplay and 72.59% after 15 min (Protoss vs. Protoss). In [15], the best accuracy reported for the separate model on Terran vs. Terran matches is 63.5%, but it was only trained on 298 matches.

In this work, we also use human vs. human replays which we processed via the SC2LE framework. We were however able to collect a larger dataset. Additionally, we avoid using rollout-based measures, so that the model is computationally efficient and can be used within a real-time SC2 agent to evaluate possible game states. For this purpose, in contrast to the existing literature, we also do not assume a fully observable game state. We however investigate how this limitation affects model performance.

A third, more recent paper using the dataset from [16] again, investigates how early winner predictions can be made [2]. It also assumes fully observable game states, but they abstain from using simulation-based measures and do not aggregate the obtained features. They are still able to achieve high prediction accuracies of over 80% after only 5 min with a KNN model. We therefore include a KNN in our comparison as well.

In addition, other types of predictions were tackled in the context of StarCraft and StarCraft II, such as army combat outcomes [19], the opponent's technology tree [1] and a player's league [3]. Winner prediction was tackled in other games as well, for example in MOBAs [23]. However, as we do not intend to develop new prediction techniques in this paper, we do not give a detailed overview of related work for other games.

2.3   Research Questions

Based on the limitations and future work directions described in the papers listed in the previous section, we formulate several research questions regarding (A) prediction accuracy and (B) interpretability of trained models.

A1 *Are specific models particularly (un-)suitable for this problem?*
   Previous studies introduce several model types. How effective are they in our problem setting?

A2 *How important is opponent information?*
   Studies such as [2] obtain high accuracies with full observability. Are these
   results transferable to our problem setting?
A3 *How important is information on game progress?*
   [22] suggests it should improve accuracy. Is that true?
B1 *Are resulting models interpretable by (expert) human players?*
   Can these models inform game designers and players?
B2 *Can (expert) human players identify indicators for outcome?*
   Some features in related work [10] incorporate expert information. How does
   this effect performance? How best to integrate it?

3   Experimental Setup

In Sect. 4, we will present the results of several experiments designed to investigate the previously stated research questions. In the following, we describe our
experimental setup. All experiments rely on training machine learning classifiers
using supervised learning. We describe the models used in Sect. 3.4, as well as
how we collect and preprocess the data required for training (see Sects. 3.1 and
3.2, respectively). In Sect. 3.3, we characterise the obtained data in more detail,
specifically by discussing the obtained features, to facilitate interpretation of the
results.

The interpretation and subsumption of results is done by an expert StarCraft
II Terran player. He competed in the European Grandmaster league (16/17)
and analyses the success of different play styles in his function as game coach.[7].
Whenever we refer to an expert opinion in the following, we describe the opinion
of this particular player.

3.1   Data Collection

The data utilized in our experiments was extracted from replays randomly
selected from the dataset published by Blizzard together with the SC2LE [22]. In
order to streamline our analysis, we chose to focus on Terran vs. Terran match-
ups exclusively (TvT in the following). This has the added benefit of being our
expert's main area of expertise.

For each selected replay, we recorded its metadata using the s2protocol library
(see Sect. 2.1). In order to obtain information on the progression of the game,
we then added details on the players' progress with a modified replay.py script
from the pysc2 library. The script outputs all available observations (cf. Sect. 3.3)
every 224 gameticks, which translates to about 10 s of gameplay.

Using this method, we were able to collect information on 4899 TvT games.
We then processed the collected information with R, thus generating datasets
characterising the players' progress for each recorded gametick, i.e. every 10 s
starting from 10 s. The longest game we recorded ended after 1:53:30 h. Additionally, we also compiled a dataset containing information of all games at their
respective last gametick.

---

[7] https://www.gamersensei.com/senseis/mperorm.

3.2 Preprocessing

A detailed look at the collected data made the need for preprocessing obvious. Since the dataset is comprised of real-world data, it contains a considerable amount of instances where players left and thus lost due to reasons not reflected in their game progress. For example, after watching some replays, we observed examples where players were idle when the game started and others, where players lost on purpose by destroying their own buildings. Since this behaviour is arguably not explainable by the collected data and would bias the trained models, we sought to remove the corresponding replays from the datasets. Based on discussion with the expert player, we thus remove games

1. in which at least one player performed 0 actions per minute,
2. that lasted 30 s or less,
3. where at least one player spent less than 50 minerals and already destroyed one of their own buildings.

Condition (1) removes games where at least one player was not active. (2) removes games where one player was not active, returned late to their PC and conceded before enemy contact was possible. (3) removes games where a player self-destructs intentionally, as friendly fire is not a sensible strategy until later in the game. The latter behaviour might be observed if players intentionally want to lower their player rating.

Within this preprocessing step, we removed 870 games, leaving us with 4029. Of the remaining games, only 17 were a tie, i.e. less than 0.5%. We therefore also removed all tied games, as they are highly uncharacteristic and our dataset does not contain enough examples to train a predictor. After preprocessing, our dataset contains data on both players of 4012 TvT replays.

3.3 Data Characterisation

From the recorded observations, we excluded features that contain no information due to game logic-based reasons (i.e. information on upgrades, shields, energy and warp gates, but also race) as well as such features that would not be available during a game, such as player performance statistics (`apm` and `mmr`) and game duration. Due to our choice of models, we also removed all discrete features (`map name`). Furthermore, we removed features that did not vary (`base build`, `score type`). The remaining features are listed in the following, presented as Cartesian products, i.e. $\{A\}x\{B\} = \{(a,b)|a \in A, b \in B\}$.

`gameloop, army count, score`
$\{\emptyset$, `collected, collection rate, spent`$\}$ x $\{$`minerals, vespene`$\}$
$\{$`friendly fire, lost, killed, used, total used`$\}$ x $\{$`minerals, vespene`$\}$
    x $\{$`none, army, economy, technology`$\}$
$\{$`total value, killed value`$\}$ x $\{$`structures, units`$\}$
$\{$`total`$\}$ x $\{$`damage dealt, damage taken, healed`$\}$ x $\{$`life`$\}$
$\{$`food`$\}$ x $\{$`workers, used army, used economy, used`$\}$
$\{$`idle`$\}$ x $\{$`production time, worker time, worker count`$\}$

They mainly contain information on resource collection, usage and destruction, as well as units and structures, food supply, idle times, and damage. The features are similar to those presented in the game observation screen and represent a player's progress in different areas of the game (e.g. army vs. economy). Other features are intended to reflect a player's efficiency (e.g. information on idleness). The features also include some information on the consequences of the opponent's actions (e.g. damage taken, resources lost). They do not, however, include spatial data, nor any reflection on observations made by scouting. As such, they are all easily available to a player or bot within a game.

3.4   Prediction Methods

Basically, we treat winner prediction as a binary classification problem, and there are of course many available methods for this, as it is one of the two fundamental activities in machine learning (the other one is regression). However, we restrict ourselves to four well-known algorithms here. One could, e.g., add Support Vector Machines or other methods, but we do not expect very different results. We have performed some manual parameter testing to configure the algorithms. However, performance differences due to parametrisation seem to be small in all cases.

Decision Trees. Recursive partitioning [4] produces (usually binary) decision trees that use simple rules for splitting the remaining data set into two parts by means of a one variable condition at every node. Interpreted graphically, this means that every decision represents a horizontal or vertical split through the decision space, which is quite restrictive concerning the obtainable partitions. However, the advantage of this method is that it can produce interpretable models, even for people with limited knowledge of machine learning. We employ the R package `rpart` with the following control parameters:
`minsplit=20, cp=0.001, maxcompete=4, maxsurrogate=10,`
`usesurrogate=2, xval=30, surrogatestyle=1, maxdepth=4`

KNN. (k-)Nearest neighbour methods work by utilising similarities between existing data points. In principle, k may be any positive number, this is the number of data points nearest to a new point that is used to decide how to classify it. In its simplest case (1nn classification), we are looking only for the nearest neighbour according to a distance function defined over the decision space, and the new point then gets the same label as this neighbour. For $k > 1$, the decision can be taken by majority vote or any other decision rule.

We utilize the `knn` method from the R package `class`, with k set to 3 and l to 0. Note that these algorithms do not possess a training step, they are computed directly.

Random Forests. This is an ensemble method based on decision trees, where different subsets of data and features are used to learn a large number (typically

500) of decision trees which are then simultaneously used for classifying a new data set by means of a voting scheme. The graphical interpretation of random forests is similar to the one of decision trees, but much more fine-grained. Much more complex surfaces can be approximated. For example, a line that is not axis-parallel can be produced by simply putting many small lines together that are shifted only by one pixel. On the other hand, it is of course much more difficult to explain how a specific random forest actually makes decisions. One can of course measure how important single features are, but this does not provide any information on how they interact. More complex approaches are needed here to identify meaningful features and their attribution [13].

In our experiments, we use the default parametrization (500 trees) of the R method `randomForest` in a package of the same name.

Artificial Neural Networks. These are the predecessors of the currently popular deep neural networks, being somewhat simpler (and usually smaller) in structure. They also lack special layer types for processing graphical data, known as convolutional layers. However, the basic working principle is the same. The network consists of nodes that can have multiple inputs and outputs, and each of these edges carries a weight. Within a node, an activation function (and maybe a bias) is used to compute the output according to the weighted sum of the input values. The weights are adapted during training in order to minimize the error, usually by means of a method named backpropagation. It is a greedy optimization procedure (following the local gradient according to the partial derivative). In principle, ANNs with at least 3 layers can learn all types of existing functions. However, for complex functions, they may require a lot of training and a large number of nodes, which in turn requires sophisticated methods to enable interpretation [13].

In our experiments, we only use a very small ANN with a single hidden layer with 7 nodes trained for 1000 iterations, implemented using the R package `nnet`. The parameters were determined using a simple grid search as well as based on observed convergence behaviour.

3.5 Training

All experiments are executed using the same settings for model training/computation. The available data is split, so that 90% of it is used for training and 10% for validation, as is done in [22]. Like in [8], the data is split per game, to ensure a fair evaluation. This way, we prevent instances, where data from the same game, e.g. from different players or gameticks, is contained in both training and test set.

We test our models for playtimes of 5–20 min, as these are characteristic game lengths and this timeframe is comparable with related work, such as [2,8]. In addition, we also investigate the final stages of play, as in [15]. The prediction accuracies are computed using 10% hold-outs in 30 independent runs on a HPC cluster (LIDO2). A single evaluation of a model for all gameticks took between a few minutes and 4 h, depending on the model and the settings.

4   Experimental Analysis

In the following, we describe the experiments and results for each of the research questions in Sect. 2.3. Most results are visualised in Fig. 1. The graphs show the prediction accuracies of different models, where the experimental settings are encoded as linetype (legend on top-left corners) and the model type as colour (legend in caption). The values displayed are the mean accuracies as well as mean accuracy ± 1.5 standard deviation in a slightly lighter colour. Plot Fig. 1(b) shows a parallel plot of different experiments, while all others show behaviour in relation to the amount of observed gametime.

The different experiments are set up by varying different parameters that slightly modify the dataset used for training and testing. The parameters we are using are listed in the following, with default values in bold.

    fs `feature selection`: {**all**, `expert`, `expert2`}
both `both players?` : {`true`, **false**}
  tw `time window`: $\mathbb{N}_0$ **(0)**
  da `data aggregation`: {**NA**, `none`, `trend`, `combined`}

Feature selection `fs` is usually set to `all`, meaning all features described in Sect. 3.3. We have also created additional feature selection methods that only select a subset of the available features based on which ones our expert player deemed to be good indicators of the outcome. A detailed description of selected features can be found in the following (paragraph *B2*). With parameter `both`, data from the second player can be included or excluded. It is important to note that if `both=t`, data from the players is included separately. Therefore, there is no obvious connection between the two players in a game, and the resulting model is thus still embodied. However, in order to avoid any correlations between samples, we usually only include the data collected for one player.

The `time window` specifies how much historic data is available to the model. For example, if `tw=2` and we are training models after 10 min of gameplay, the data from 9:40 min and 9:50 min would be available as well. By default, however, only the gametick in question is available. The additional historic data is added after being transformed by a data aggregation method `da`. More details on the data aggregation methods tested can be found in the following (paragraph *A3*).

We also want to note that the implementation of the ANN model only allows for a limited amount of features. For this reason, this model failed to run for a few of the settings discussed in the following. In these cases, the corresponding runs are excluded from the results and do not appear in the figures. The KNN model computation timed out (8 h) for one experiment setting and is thus not included in the corresponding plot.

In the following, we interpret our experimental results in the light of the research questions formulated in Sect. 2.3 (A1, A2, A3, B1, B2).

A1: Model Comparison. In most of the work referenced in Sect. 2, several prediction models were tested. In our study, we are therefore looking to apply the best performing model types, i.e. KNNs in [2] and ANNs in [22] to our problem

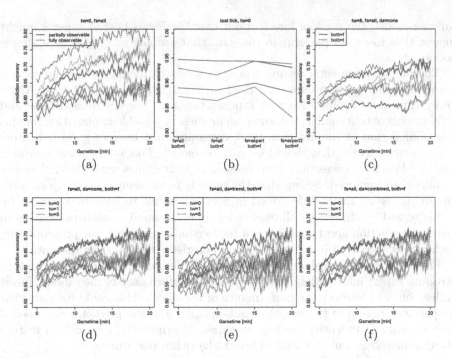

Fig. 1. Prediction accuracy with different methods (a), at the end of the game with different features (b), with and w/o both players datasets (c), and with different types of historic information (d–f), over the most interesting game period (not (b)). Prediction methods: • Decision tree, • ANN, • Random Forest, • KNN. (Color figure online)

setting. We focus on simple and small models as well as ones that are likely interpretable, such as decision trees. For more details on the models and their implementation in our analysis, see Sect. 3.4.

We have executed all experiments described above for a • decision tree, • ANN, • random forest, and • KNN model. The achieved accuracies are displayed in the respective graphs in Fig. 1. We observe that random forests perform well in general and achieve the best performance in most settings. Except for the experiment visualised in Fig. 1(b), the decision tree and ANN have similar performance. In contrast to the expectations resulting from its stellar performance in [2], our KNN model has the weakest performance in most of our tests. However, the dataset the models in [2] were trained on are significantly smaller than ours. It is also important to note that the random forest and ANN models in particular could benefit from an even larger dataset.

Except for in the experiment on the last gametick displayed in Fig. 1(b), all models seem to react similarly to additional or modified data. This means the performance improves and decreases for the same experimental settings by roughly the same amount. The algorithms also display very similar scaling behaviour with an increasing length of observed gametime. Therefore, different approaches should be tested in the future. Additionally, the fact that the most complex model, the random forest in our case, performs best in general, might suggest that there are patterns in the data that are not picked up by a simple model.

The only experimental setting where this relative behaviour of the models is not displayed are the ones visualised in Fig. 1(b). For the last tick, ANNs are in some cases competitive with random forests, while the decision tree and KNN models obtain similar, but lower accuracies. A possible explanation for this behaviour is that at the last tick, there certainly must be very good indicators of the game outcome that should be easy to model. This is of course assuming that the data was successfully preprocessed so that games with external causes of conceit are removed. Seeing that the models reach accuracies of up to 95%, our preprocessing method described in Sect. 3.2 seems to have been successful in this regard. Additionally, all models have only a small standard deviation in terms of prediction accuracy. This is a further indication that our preprocessing method was successful in removing uncharacteristic outliers from the dataset.

Furthermore, we can observe that using different feature selection methods to introduce expert information barely affects the performance of the random forest models, but can improve the performance of all others. This could indicate that the parametrisation of the models is sub-optimal and the predictor e.g. needed more iterations to identify the best features. Alternatively, data-driven feature selection methods could be used to boost algorithm performance.

Overall, we achieve competitive performance to the related work described in Sect. 2.2. We were able to improve the results presented in [22], the most comparable experimental setup, in terms of early prediction accuracy by around 5% at the 8 min mark. We achieved similar accuracies after 20 min of gametime (around 70%), even with our considerably less complex modelling approach. Improvements in terms of earlier prediction can also be observed when compared to [8]. We have also achieved better results than the TvT win predictor reported on in [15], but we had access to more data. We are, however, not able to reproduce the extremely high prediction accuracies obtained in [2], even when assuming complete observability (see below).

A2: Observability. Much of the work described in Sect. 2.2 allows fully observable game states instead of our embodied perspective. In the following, we therefore investigate how much the observability of the opponent's behaviour affects prediction accuracy. In Fig. 1(a), we visualise the performance improvement of our models when information on the opponent is added. To do this, we train the models on a modified dataset where each sample contains all features Sect. 3.3 for both players at the same time. All of the trained models show a significant improvement of between 2–10%, depending on model and gametick.

This shows that the results from papers with the assumption of fully observable game states are definitely not directly transferable to our situation and work on embodied outcome prediction is therefore still necessary. This result also seems to suggest that a suitable use of the scouting mechanics available to players in StarCraft II will improve a player's capacity for assessing their own chances of winning. Furthermore, the fact that information on a single player's progress is not sufficient to explain the outcome, strongly suggests that no strategy exists that dominates all others. Otherwise, the winner of a game would always be the player that best executed the dominating strategy. Instead, the players seem to have multiple viable strategies available. This is even more remarkable since we only analyse Terran vs Terran games. This was probably intended by the game designers [5].

A3: Historic Data. The authors of [22] presume that prediction accuracy can be significantly improved if it was based on more than just the observations at a given time. This sentiment was echoed by our expert player. We therefore investigate different ways to include information on previous gameticks in the data. We compare the case where no historic data is used (tw=0), only the previous observation is used (tw=1) and one where we look as far back as a minute (tw=5). For each of these different settings of tw, we also experiment with different aggregation methods of the data da. If the time window is set to 0, this parameter is obviously not meaningful and is thus usually set to NA. If tw $\neq$ 0, however, historic data is either inserted as independent samples (none), combined into a single sample (combined) or the observed trend (trend) is computed (as the mean of consecutive differences of the observed values per feature). While we do not encode any domain knowledge with none, we provide a bit more information to the models. With combined we suggest a potential correlation of the values and with trend, we specifically force the model to focus on trend information.

The results are displayed in Figs. 1(d)–(f). Surprisingly, for da=none and da=combined, we cannot observe a performance improvement when adding historic data. In fact, the performance even seems to decrease for da=trend. The latter might be a result of the specific modelling of the trend we chose in this case, but the results are still unexpected. They could potentially be explained by the fact that we have only recorded observations every 10 s of the game. This limitation might not have been differentiated enough, as units are usually killed and reproduced within very short time spans. However, this is generally not true for (important) structures. Another potential reason could be that the complexity of the relationship between historic and current data could not be represented by our simple models and given a relatively small amount of data. Given more data, deep learning approaches (especially those intended to capture trends in data) might be better suited for this experiment and have a potential to improve the results.

B1: Interpretability. In the following, we anecdotally investigate the interpretability of our decision tree models, as they are the most suitable approach for this analysis. To do this, we have generated decision trees for various scenarios, namely

- Last tick prediction with expert features
- Prediction after 10 min with expert features

- Prediction after 10 min, with expert features, but using historic data (trend aggregations)
- Prediction after 10 min, with all features, but using historic data (trend aggregations)

The resulting models are depicted in Fig. 2. See also paragraph *B2* for more details on the feature sets. They were able to obtain prediction accuracies of approximately 0.898, 0.67, 0.556, 0.595, respectively. The last three models depict the data observed at the same point in time and were generated from the same split of training and test data to facilitate a comparison.

It is important to note, that studies suggest that non-experts can only simultaneously grasp 5–9 different variables with 3–15 values [12]. Therefore, to guarantee interpretability, the features would need to be discretised. Additionally, the decision should be parameterised accordingly to prevent generating too many branches. Interestingly, the decision tree trained on data containing all features (i.e. `fs=all`), instead of just a subset, comes closest to the mentioned constraints of interpretability.

Despite this caveat, we asked our human expert player to interpret the models, as they still contain interpretable information when focusing on different branches separately. According to him, the first model seems very reasonable in context of the game. It asks if the player has any army left. If not, then it tries to assess with damage taken and dealt, whether the opponent has any army left either. A human player would probably look at similar statistics.

The second model appears to be quite similar. What stands out as unexpected, is that both models use the number of idle workers. One possible interpretation is that players have many idle workers if there is an imminent and critical threat, which forces the player to pull their workers away from mining. A large number of idle workers also indicates a non-efficient management of resources and build order.

The third model seems much closer to the approach a human would take to evaluate their chances of winning, i.e. interpret the trends in game data. If the amount of damage done increases and the amount of damage taken does not increase significantly in a time frame of 10 s (`tw=1`), this indicates the player won a battle. Of course, a won battle generates a strong advantage over the other player at that point in time. If the collection-rate increases compared to the last observed game state, the player was able to expand their economy without being punished for it. This is another indicator of success and can be interpreted as a sign that winning chances are good.

Tree number 4 seems reasonable as well. However, resource production, which is used as the main feature here, is very dependent on the strategy and thus not an ideal predictor, especially with partial info. Furthermore, while resource production is an important part, it is more telling how efficiently they are used for military and economy (`resources_spent`). This is because gathering resources is relatively easy, the more difficult skill is developing and executing a good and adaptive build order. Further down the tree, however, the distinctions are comparable to the previous trees.

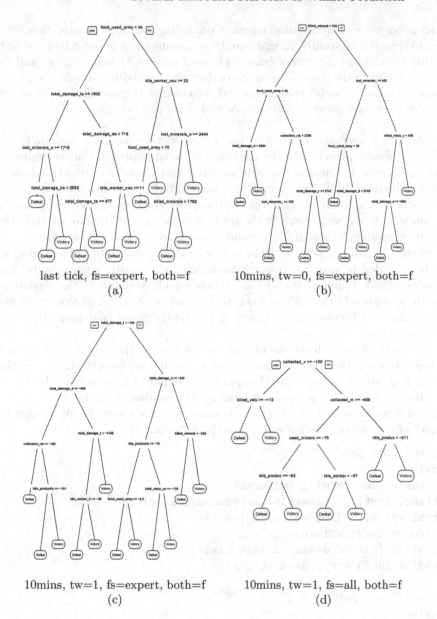

last tick, fs=expert, both=f
(a)

10mins, tw=0, fs=expert, both=f
(b)

10mins, tw=1, fs=expert, both=f
(c)

10mins, tw=1, fs=all, both=f
(d)

Fig. 2. Decision trees learned for the last tick (a) and for the game state after 10 min (b–d) as samples for checking differences between machine learning based and expert human reasoning.

Overall, according to the expert, it is hard to understand why model 3 has a comparably weak prediction rate, as it definitely is the most human-like approach. However, it is also surprising that predictions on the game state can be so good with so little information. Concluding, while there are caveats to the interpretability from a formal standpoint, some models seem to be able to capture the thought process of (expert) human players. Others seem to find different patterns in the data. This suggests that after applying suitable complexity constraints and a careful evaluation and selection of the specific model to use, decision trees have potential to be used to inform players.

B2: Domain Knowledge. Finally, we investigate ways to integrate domain knowledge from expert players into the models. This is an approach that is commonly used in industry, but also in research (see Sect. 2.2), in order to bias the machine learning model suitably. In our case, we chose to test restricting the search space for model training, hoping that this will improve the convergence properties of the models. At the same time, it should reduce the risk of the models reflecting non-interpretable data artifacts instead of underlying game characteristics.

From a human perspective, there is an extraordinary amount of features that can be recorded by the SC2 research framework to describe a game state. This includes all sorts of information from features readily available to the player such as supply (known in the API as food) to information that no player would ever have a chance of keeping track of, such as the total amount of damage they have dealt in a match.

For many of these features, players would assume that they carry little to no information related to the outcome of a match. Our expert player has thus chosen two sets of features called `expert` and `expert2` from the available ones described in Sect. 3.3, the second set being even smaller than the first one. The selected features were deemed to be the most important ones for predicting the winner of the match. They are listed in the following:

Expert Feature Set:
```
gameloop
{∅, collection rate} x {minerals}
{killed, lost} x {minerals} x {economy, army}
{total value, killed value} x {units}
killed value structures
{total} x {damage dealt, damage taken} x {life}
{food} x {used army, used economy}
```

Expert2 Feature Set:
```
gameloop
{killed, lost} x {minerals} x {economy, army}
{total value, killed value} x {units}
{food} x {army, workers}
```

Food_army, the amount of supply currently spent on army, was chosen as it directly correlates with a player's army size. If a player has little to no army, especially in later stages of the game, this is a strong indicator that they are losing. Food_workers can also be a strong indica-

tor of whether a player is winning or losing. If the player has few workers left, they will not be able to rebuild an army, and thus risk losing if
their army is destroyed. Killed_minerals_army, killed_minerals_economy,
lost_minerals_army, and lost_minerals_economy were chosen as they can be
used to gauge which player won the battles. This is because these features allow
some information on the success of the opposing player. If a player has killed
significantly more minerals than they have lost, they are certainly in a favorable
position.

Killed_value_structures was chosen as a clear indicator of a critical situation
in the game. Players generally do not lose many structures.

It is important to note that the selected features do not necessarily coincide
with the features identified as most important by our models (cf. decision tree 4
in Fig. 2). A larger scale study on the usage of features by the different models
would be needed to allow general statements on feature selection. However, we
can observe the influence of restricting the feature sets on the models. The
corresponding plot can be found in Fig. 1(b).

The effect of this approach to integrating domain knowledge seems to depend
heavily on the model type and is not necessarily positive. This finding demonstrates the difficulties of suitably biasing general machine learning approaches
to improve their performance. In our experiments, restricting the search space
did definitely decrease the computation time, however. From our data, we cannot conclude whether a strictly data-based approach with more complex models
and larger amounts of data is more promising than identifying better ways to
integrate domain knowledge. Both appear to offer potential for improving the
prediction models.

In the following, we thus take a different approach to assessing domain knowledge. Our expert player has attempted to go through his own replays to find scenarios, where either predicting the winner was easy or he failed to do so. Based
on this information, we outline how human players approach the subject of estimating the likelihood of winning independent of our models. In one instance,
the outcome was reportedly easy to tell based on information gathered from
contacts with the opposing player. It is however unclear how this information
is reflected in the features we collected in our study. Deep learning approaches
trained on raw information collected from the minimap as done in [22] might be
able to capture this. Our data would only reflect the trades made for buildings
and military.

In scenarios where these trades are obvious, a predictor is likely able to pick
up on them. However, since units and structures are encoded via their resource
value in the recorded data, this can only be interpreted in a meaningful way if the
resource values accurately reflect the value of the unit or building in the game.
This is unlikely, because the value of certain units depends on the strategy of the
opponent. Instead, this issue could be approached by counting the number of
different units and structures individually, so that the tradeoffs can be identified
via data analysis. Different units have been encoded separately in [2] (mostly
by type, e.g. air and ground units). But this approach increases the number of

features, which reduces the interpretability of the resulting models, which is why it was avoided in this study.

An interesting avenue to characterising the difference between our trained model predictors and human experience would be to identify enough replays that are similar to scenarios where winner prediction is easy or hard for human players. The models could then be used to evaluate the corresponding replays to assess whether data-driven approaches could be used as information tools for pro-players in these specific cases.

5   Conclusion and Outlook

In this paper, we have approached embodied winner prediction in StarCraft II as a machine learning problem using replays collected and published by Blizzard and DeepMind [22]. We were able to achieve competitive results, even with

- simple, interpretable models
- with simple features
- on human vs. human data.

While there is still potential for improvement of the respective models, finding the best predictor was not the intent of this paper. Instead, we focus on investigating which directions of future research suggested in previous work seem most promising. To this end, we identify several research questions, mostly targeted towards the influence of observability and other information constraints on achievable prediction accuracy. Furthermore, we give a detailed description of our preprocessing method as well as a baseline accuracy for embodied winner prediction in StarCraft II.

We demonstrate that while adding information on the opposing player can facilitate the prediction of the winner, this is not necessarily true when adding information on previous game states instead. This was a surprising result, but it is possible that different methods of integration or a larger amount of data might produce different results. Furthermore, we find that biasing trained models with domain knowledge does also not necessarily translate into improved performance. Finally, while we are able to produce models that contain information comprehensible to an (expert) human player, more work is required to guarantee and investigate interpretability.

Therefore, in the future, more research is required concerning different ways of integrating different types of information into data-driven prediction models. This is true for additional information and interpretative measures based on domain knowledge (such as LTD2 [10] and the expression of strategy in [15]), as well as for information gathered from previously made observations in the same game. More work is also required towards formal definitions on the interpretability of trained models for complex games. Frameworks that allow the visual exploration of different features and their attribution [13] are a promising approach to make even more complex models interpretable. Alternatively, the feature space a more complex model learns can also be used as a proxy task to train simpler models on. This way, knowledge can be distilled into a less complex model [9].

In terms of improvement of the achieved prediction accuracies, increasing the complexity of the models as well as the amount and complexity of training data (by adding more replays, but also spatial data) appears to be a promising approach with hopefully interesting newly discovered patterns in the data. Another way of enhancing the data is to include more historic data. A thusly enhanced data set might even allow the use of deep learning models that are potentially able to uncover more complexities. We ran preliminary tests with deep learning models on the existing data, which did not improve the obtained prediction accuracies. But, given more or enhanced data, these methods definitely have potential.

We, however, want to concentrate our future efforts on transferring our findings on winner prediction to approaches on game state evaluation. While this would certainly be an interesting topic for future StarCraft II AI research, we want to focus more on its application to AI-assisted game design to express aspects such as drama or decisiveness [6].

References

1. Alburg, H., et al.: Making and Acting on Predictions in StarCraft: Brood War. University of Gothenburg (2014)
2. Álvarez-Caballero, A., et al.: Early prediction of the winner in StarCraft matches. In: International Joint Conference on Computational Intelligence (2017)
3. Avontuur, T., Spronck, P., van Zaanen, M.: Player skill modeling in Starcraft II. In: Ninth AAAI Conference on Artificial Intelligence and Interactive Digital Entertainment, Boston, MA, USA, pp. 2–8. AAAI Press (2014)
4. Breiman, L., et al.: Classiffication and Regression Trees. Wadsworth and Brooks, Monterey (1984)
5. Browder, D.: The game design of STARCRAFT II: designing an E-Sport. In: Game Developers Conference (GDC) (2011). http://www.gdcvault.com/play/1014488/The-Game-Design-of-STARCRAFT
6. Browne, C., Maire, F.: Evolutionary game design. IEEE Trans. Comput. Intell. AI Games 2(1), 1–16 (2010)
7. Browne, C.B., et al.: A survey of monte carlo tree search methods. IEEE Trans. Comput. Intell. AI Games 4(1), 1–43 (2012)
8. Erickson, G., Buro, M.: Global state evaluation in StarCraft. In: AAAI Conference on Artificial Intelligence and Interactive Digital Entertainment, pp. 112–118 (2014)
9. Hinton, G.E., Vinyals, O., Dean, J.: Distilling the knowledge in a neural network. In: NIPS Deep Learning Workshop (2014). https://arxiv.org/abs/1503.02531
10. Kovarsky, A., Buro, M.: Heuristic search applied to abstract combat games. In: Kégl, B., Lapalme, G. (eds.) AI 2005. LNCS (LNAI), vol. 3501, pp. 66–78. Springer, Heidelberg (2005). https://doi.org/10.1007/11424918_9
11. Lopes, R., Bidarra, R.: Adaptivity challenges in games and simulations: a survey. IEEE Trans. Comput. Intell. AI Games 3(2), 85–99 (2011)
12. Miller, G.: The magical number seven, plus or minus two: some limits on our capacity for processing information. Psychol. Rev. 63, 81–97 (1956)

13. Olah, C., et al.: The building blocks of interpretability. Distill (2018). https:// distill.pub/2018/building-blocks
14. Perez-Liebana, D., et al.: General video game AI: competition, challenges and opportunities. In: AAAI Conference on Artificial Intelligence, pp. 4335–4337 (2016)
15. Ravari, Y.N., Bakkes, S., Spronck, P.: StarCraft winner prediction. In: AAAI Conference on Artificial Intelligence and Interactive Digital Entertainment (2016)
16. Robertson, G., Watson, I.D.: An improved dataset and extraction process for Starcraft AI. In: FLAIRS Conference, pp. 255–260 (2014)
17. Sánchez-Ruiz-Granados, A.A.: Predicting the winner in two player StarCraft games. In: CoSECivi, pp. 24–35 (2015)
18. Stanescu, M., et al.: Evaluating real-time strategy game states using convolutional neural networks. In: IEEE Conference on Computational Intelligence and Games (2016)
19. Stanescu, M., et al.: Predicting army combat outcomes in StarCraft. In: AAAI Conference on Artificial Intelligence and Interactive Digital Entertainment, pp. 86–92 (2013)
20. Summerville, A., et al.: Understanding mario: an evaluation of design metrics for platformers. In: Foundations of Digital Games. ACM, New York (2017)
21. Čertický, M., Churchill, D.: The current state of StarCraft AI competitions and bots. In: Artificial Intelligence and Interactive Digital Entertainment Conference (2017)
22. Vinyals, O., et al.: StarCraft II: A New Challenge for Reinforcement Learning. CoRR abs/1708.04782 (2017). arXiv: 1708.04782
23. Yang, P., Harrison, B.E., Roberts, D.L.: Identifying patterns in combat that are predictive of success in MOBA games. In: Foundations of Digital Games (2014)

MOBA-Slice: A Time Slice Based Evaluation Framework of Relative Advantage Between Teams in MOBA Games

Lijun Yu[1,2(✉)], Dawei Zhang[2], Xiangqun Chen[1], and Xing Xie[2]

[1] Peking University, Beijing, China
yulijun@pku.edu.cn, cherry@sei.pku.edu.cn
[2] Microsoft Research Asia, Beijing, China
zhangdawei@outlook.com, xing.xie@microsoft.com

Abstract. Multiplayer Online Battle Arena (MOBA) is currently one of the most popular genres of digital games around the world. The domain of knowledge contained in these complicated games is large. It is hard for humans and algorithms to evaluate the real-time game situation or predict the game result. In this paper, we introduce **MOBA-Slice**, a time slice based evaluation framework of relative advantage between teams in MOBA games. MOBA-Slice is a quantitative evaluation method based on learning, similar to the value network of AlphaGo. It establishes a foundation for further MOBA related research including AI development. In MOBA-Slice, with an analysis of the deciding factors of MOBA game results, we design a neural network model to fit our discounted evaluation function. Then we apply MOBA-Slice to Defense of the Ancients 2 (DotA2), a typical and popular MOBA game. Experiments on a large number of match replays show that our model works well on arbitrary matches. MOBA-Slice not only has an accuracy 3.7% higher than DotA Plus Assistant (A subscription service provided by DotA2) at result prediction, but also supports the prediction of the remaining time of a game, and then realizes the evaluation of relative advantage between teams.

Keywords: Computer games · Applications of supervised learning · Game playing and machine learning

1 Introduction

Multiplayer Online Battle Arena (MOBA) is a sub-genre of strategy video games. Players of two teams each control a playable character competing to destroy the opposing team's main structure, with the assistance of periodically spawned computer-controlled units. Figure 1(a)[1] is a typical map of a MOBA genre game. MOBA is currently one of the most popular genres of digital games around

---

[1] https://en.wikipedia.org/wiki/File:Map_of_MOBA.svg

© Springer Nature Switzerland AG 2019
T. Cazenave et al. (Eds.): CGW 2018, CCIS 1017, pp. 23–40, 2019.
https://doi.org/10.1007/978-3-030-24337-1_2

the world. Among championships of MOBA globally, Defense of the Ancients 2 (DotA2) has the most generously awarded tournaments. DotA2 is a typical MOBA game in which two teams of five players collectively destroy enemy's structure, Ancient, while defending their own. The playable characters are called heroes, each of which has its unique design, strengths, and weaknesses. The two teams, Radiant and Dire, occupy fortified bases called plateau in opposite corners of the map as Fig. 1(b)[2] shows.

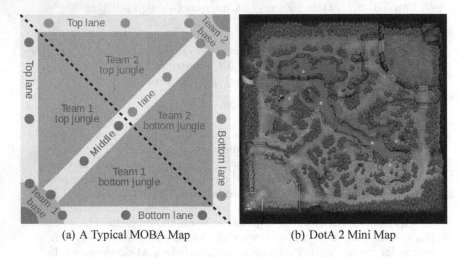

(a) A Typical MOBA Map   (b) DotA 2 Mini Map

Fig. 1. Maps

In games with a scoring mechanism, we can easily tell which player or team has an advantage from the scores. But the design of MOBA games such as DotA2 is complicated, with lots of variables changing during the whole game. So it is hard to evaluate the real-time game situation in such a large domain of knowledge. Traditionally, players and commentators assess the relative advantage by intuitive feeling, their own experience and fuzzy methods. No unified standard has been proposed, to the best of our knowledge. Such evaluation is needed in further research related to MOBA. It plays an essential role in developing artificial intelligence for MOBA games, such as working as the reward function in reinforcement learning models [20] or the evaluation function in Monte Carlo planning models [5]. In strategy analysis, the effectiveness of strategies can also be estimated by the change of relative advantage between teams.

In this paper, we introduce MOBA-Slice, which is able to evaluate any time slice of a game quantitatively. Different from manually designed evaluation function, MOBA-Slice provides a model that learns from data, which is similar to the value network of AlphaGo [18]. It establishes a foundation for further MOBA related research including AI development and strategy analysis.

The main contribution of this paper is listed below.

---

[2] https://dota2.gamepedia.com/File:Minimap_7.07.png.

1. *We introduce MOBA-Slice, a time slice based evaluation framework of relative advantage between teams in MOBA games.* We analyze the deciding factors of MOBA game result. A discounted evaluation function is defined to compute the relative advantage. We design a supervised learning model based on Neural Network to do this evaluation. MOBA-Slice is able to predict the result and remaining time of ongoing matches.
2. *We apply MOBA-Slice to DotA2 and prove the effectiveness of MOBA-Slice with experiments.* We embody MOBA-Slice on a typical MOBA game, DotA2. We process a large number of DotA2 match replays to train our model. Experiments show that the model is able to evaluate time slices of arbitrary DotA2 matches. In the aspect of predicting the game result, MOBA-Slice has an accuracy 3.7% higher than DotA Plus Assistant.

2   MOBA-Slice

2.1   MOBA Game Result Analysis

In a MOBA game, the final victory is of the most significance. MOBA Game Result (**MGR**) analysis is defined to describe the deciding factors of the result of a match. For a certain time point, the future result of the game is considered related to two aspects, current state and future trend. The current state describes the game situation at this specific time slice, which is the foundation of future development. The future trend represents how the match will develop from the current state. Figure 2 shows the content of MGR analysis.

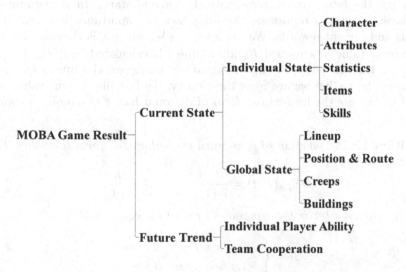

Fig. 2. MGR analysis

In details, the current state includes every information we can get to know about the game from a particular time slice. As MOBA are multiplayer games where each player controls one character, we further divide the factors of current status into individual and global state. The individual state contains the information of each character, including its type, attributes such as position and experience, statistics such as the count of deaths, the items it possesses, the skills it masters, and so on. The global state describes the background environment and the relationship between characters. The global information includes the lineup depicting the types of characters in both teams. Lineup can also reveal the advantage or disadvantage of a specific combination of characters. The position and selected route of characters, the status of creeps and buildings are considered in global state, as well. All the information mentioned above that will be used to represent current state can be found in game records, such as replay files.

Different from the current state, the part of future trend focuses on the level of players. Given the same status as a start, different players and teams will have distinct game processes and lead to various game results. We also divide this part into individual ability and team cooperation. The ability of each player individually can be measured through ranking systems such as TrueSkill [8,16]. We further include the part of team cooperation, as good members do not necessarily mean a strong team. The detailed method to evaluate team cooperation still requires further research and is not covered in this paper.

2.2 Discounted Evaluation

MGR analysis describes how the result of a match comes out, and reversely we can use the *future* result to evaluate the *current* states. In Q learning [23], the discount factor γ represents the difference in importance between future rewards and present rewards. We can let $\gamma = \frac{1}{1+r}$, where r is the discount rate. The current value of a reward R_a after time t is calculated by $\gamma^t R_a$. Inspired by this, in the evaluation of current situation, we regard the future victory as a reward. The farther we are from the victory, the less the current value of its reward is. We use the logarithmic form of discount factor to simplify exponent operation.

Definition 1. *The function of discounted evaluation DE for a time slice TS is defined as:*

$$DE_{TS}(R,t) = \frac{1}{\ln(1+r)^t} \times R = \frac{R}{\alpha t} \qquad (1)$$

where $\alpha = \ln(1+r)$, t is the remaining time of the game, and

$$R = \begin{cases} 1, \text{when Team A wins} \\ -1, \text{when Team B wins} \end{cases} \qquad (2)$$

DE_{TS} has several appealing properties:

1. The sign of its value represents the final result, positive for A's victory, negative for B's.

2. Its absolute value is inversely proportional to t.
3. The value approximately represents the advantage team A has in comparison to team B.

Here is some explanation of property 3. In normal cognition, greater advantage indicates more probability of winning, which would result in less time to end the game. So we can suppose that there is a negative correlation between the advantage gap between two teams and t. This assumption may be challenged by the intuition that the game situation fluctuates and even reverses at times. We can divide such fluctuation into random and systematic ones. The players' faults that occur randomly can be smoothed in a large scale of data. Systematic fluctuation is considered to be the result of misinterpretation of advantage. For example, in games where team A wins, if the intuitionistic advantage of team A usually gets smaller after certain time slice x, there is a reason to doubt that the advantage of team A at x is over-estimated. Traditional ways to evaluate advantage usually ignores the potential fluctuation and does not take game progress into consideration. In our method, we can suppose the absolute value of the advantage between teams keeps growing from the beginning as a small value till the end. The value of function DE_{TS} changes in the same way.

Although the values of both R and t are unknown for a current time slice in an ongoing match, we can train a supervised learning model to predict the value of function DE_{TS} for each time slice. Based on property 3, the model would be a good evaluator for relative advantage between teams.

2.3   Time Slice Evaluation Model

We intend to design a supervised learning model which takes time slices as input and outputs the value of function DE_{TS}. Due to the current limitation of research, we only consider the factors in the part of current state in MGR analysis while designing models.

The structure of this Time Slice Evaluation (**TSE**) model is shown in Fig. 3(a). TSE model contains two parts of substructures. The individual (Ind) part calculates the contribution of each character in the game separately, which corresponds to the individual state in MGR analysis. Different characters in MOBA games have distinctive design, strengths, and weaknesses. This part ignores any potential correlation between characters but learns the unique features of each character. The global (Glo) part calculates the contribution of all the characters in a match, corresponding to the global state in MGR analysis. This part takes all the characters in a match as a whole and is designed to learn the potential relationship of addition or restriction. To combine the Ind and Glo, the outputs of the two parts are fed to l_c layers of n_c neurons activated by $relu$ function [15]. The output is calculated by one neuron activated by $tanh$ function to get a result in the range $[-1, 1]$.

For a MOBA game which has c_a playable characters in total, the Ind part consists c_a parts of subnets, each of which calculates a character's contribution. For c_m characters in a time slice, we use their corresponding subnets to calculate

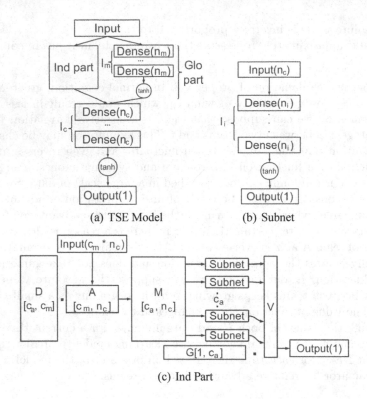

(a) TSE Model

(b) Subnet

(c) Ind Part

Fig. 3. Model structure

their contribution individually, sum for each team and then subtract team B from team A to get the final result. Usually, in MOBA games each character is not allowed to be used more than once, so each subnet is calculated at most once for a time slice. But in practice, there is still a problem for Ind part to train in batch. Different characters are used in different matches, so the outputs need to be calculated with different sets of subnets. The data path in the model varies for time slices from different matches.

With the structure defined in Fig. 3(c), batch training is implemented. If each character takes n_c dimensions of data, the input of a time slice can be reshaped into a matrix $A \in \mathbb{R}^{c_m \times n_c}$. We create a distributer matrix D for each input, which only contains c_m non-zero elements. $D[i, j] = 1$ means that the id of the i-th character in this game is j, so the i-th row of A will be at the j-th row in matrix $M = D \cdot A$ and will be fed to the j-th subnet. In vector $G \in \mathbb{R}^{1 \times c_a}$, $G[0, i] = 1$ indicates character i is in team A and $G[0, i] = -1$ indicates character i is in team B. Vector $V \in \mathbb{R}^{c_a \times 1}$ contains the output of all c_a subnets. We finally calculate the output by $output = G \cdot V$.

The subnets of Ind part are feed-forward neural networks of the same scale. Each subnet in Fig. 3(b) takes in n_c dimensions of input and outputs with a neuron activated by tanh. Each subnet has l_i hidden layers of n_i neurons activated by *relu* and applied dropout [19] at rate r_d.

The Glo part is simply a multilayer feed-forward structure. It is like the subnet of Ind part but in a much larger scale. It takes in a full time slice vector and outputs with one neuron activated by tanh. The Glo part has l_m fully connected hidden layers with each n_m neurons, activated by *relu* function and applied dropout at rate r_d.

To get better distribution, we set the output of TSE model:

$$y = \frac{1}{DE_{TS}(R,t)} = \frac{\alpha t}{R} \tag{3}$$

And it needs to be transformed to correspond to the range of tanh function:

$$y_{scaled} = -1 + 2 \times \frac{y - y_{min}}{y_{max} - y_{min}} \in [-1,1] \tag{4}$$

Let $\hat{y}$ be the prediction from model. To transform it back. we can rescale $\hat{y}$ by:

$$\hat{y}_{rescaled} = y_{min} + \frac{\hat{y}+1}{2} \times (y_{max} - y_{min}) \tag{5}$$

and then prediction of t and R can be extracted as:

$$\hat{t} = |\hat{y}_{rescaled}|/\alpha \tag{6}$$

$$\hat{R} = sign(\hat{y}_{rescaled}) \tag{7}$$

As a regression problem, mean absolute error (MAE) and mean squared error (MSE) are chosen as metrics. MAE is also the loss function. We can further calculate a rescaled MAE by

$$MAE_{rescaled}(\hat{y}, y_{scaled}) = MAE(\hat{y}, y_{scaled}) \times \frac{y_{max} - y_{min}}{2} \tag{8}$$

Lemma 1.

$$|\hat{y}_{rescaled} - y| \geq \alpha |\hat{t} - t| \tag{9}$$

Proof.

$$|\hat{y}_{rescaled} - y| = \left| \frac{\alpha \hat{t}}{\hat{R}} - \frac{\alpha t}{R} \right|$$
$$= \begin{cases} \alpha |\hat{t} - t| & \text{when } \hat{R} = R \\ \alpha |\hat{t} + t| \geq \alpha |\hat{t} - t| & \text{when } \hat{R} = -R \end{cases} \tag{10}$$

where $|R| = |\hat{R}| = 1$ and $t, \hat{t} \geq 0$

Theorem 1.

$$MAE_{rescaled}(\hat{y}, y_{scaled}) \geq \alpha MAE(\hat{t}, t) \tag{11}$$

Proof.

$$MAE_{rescaled}(\hat{y}, y_{scaled}) = MAE(\hat{y}_{rescaled}, y)$$

$$= \frac{\sum_{i=1}^{N} |\hat{y}_{rescaled} - y|}{N}$$

$$\geq \frac{\sum_{i=1}^{N} \alpha |\hat{t} - t|}{N} \tag{12}$$

$$= \alpha MAE(\hat{t}, t)$$

So $MAE_{rescaled}(\hat{y}, y_{scaled})/\alpha$ proves to be the upper bound of $MAE(t, \hat{t})$. It provides a more intuitive way to evaluate the model's effectiveness, as its value can be viewed in units of time to reveal the mean error of prediction.

3   Experiments

3.1   Apply MOBA-Slice to DotA2

We choose DotA2 as a typical MOBA game to apply MOBA-Slice. DotA2 generates a replay file to record all the information in a match. An open source parser from OpenDota project[3] can parse the replay file and generate *interval* messages every second to record the state of each character. The following information contained in *interval* messages is chosen to describe a time slice in current experiments.

- Character - hero id
- Attributes: life state, gold, experience, coordinate(x, y)
- Statistics:
  - deaths, kills, last hit, denies, assists
  - stacked creeps, stacked camps, killed towers, killed roshans
  - placed observer, placed sentry, rune pickup, team-fight participation
- Items: 244 types

There are 114 characters which are called heroes in DotA2. In a match, each team chl4 ooses five heroes without repetition. A hero may die at times and then respawn after a period of delay. The life state attribute is used to record whether a hero is alive or dead. Gold and experience are two essential attributes of a hero. Gold is primarily obtained by killing enemy heroes, destroying enemy structures and killing creeps. Heroes can use their gold to purchase items that provide special abilities. A hero's experience level begins at level 1 and grows as the game goes on. It is highly related to the level of a hero's ability. The position of a hero on the map is given in coordinate representation x and y.

Many kinds of statistics are generated automatically by the game engine and the replay parser to help analyze the game. Deaths, kills, last hit, denies and assists record these historical events during the fights. Stacked creeps, camps and killed towers, roshans record the hero's fight history regarding these units.

---

[3] Replay parser from OpenDota project: https://github.com/odota/parser.

Invisible watchers, observer and sentry, are helpful items that allow watching over areas and spy on enemies. Runes are special boosters that spawn on the game map, which enhance heroes' ability in various ways. A team-fight is a fight provoked by several players with a considerable scale. There are 244 types of items in DotA2 that can be purchased by a hero, according to our statistics.

In the aspect of global state, lineup is represented by the id of 10 heroes. Position and route are reflected in the coordinates of heroes. Since skill of heroes and status of creeps and buildings are not recorded in *interval* messages, we do not involve these fields of information in current experiments. Using lower-level parser such as manta[4] and clarity[5] to extract data from raw Protobuf structured replay is likely to address this problem, but it significantly increases the complexity of data processing.

3.2 Data Processing

The digital distribution platform developed by Valve Corporation, Steam, officially provides APIs[6] for DotA2 game statistics. We use *GetLeagueListing* and *GetMatchHistory* methods to get the list of all matches of professional game leagues[7]. We then use OpenDota's API[8] to get detailed information of matches including the URL of its replay file on Valve's servers. After downloading and decompressing them, we send replay files to OpenDota's parser. With a massive cost of CPU time, we get downloaded and parsed replay files of 105,915 matches of professional leagues, with a total size of over 3 TB.

We scan parsed replay files and create time slice vectors every 60 s of game time. In a vector, each of ten heroes has 263 dimensions, including 1 for hero id, 5 for attributes, 13 for statistics and 244 for items. Along with one dimension recording the game time, each time slice vector has 2,631 dimensions. We also generate the value of function DE_{TS} for each time slice, with the already known game result. In this process, we notice that about 34 thousand replays are not correctly parsed due to game version issues, file corruption or known limitation of the parser. After dropping these invalid data, we get 2,802,329 time slices generated from 71,355 matches. The distribution of match length is shown in Fig. 4. The average length is about 40 min, with few matches shorter than 10 min and very few matches longer than 100 min.

3.3 First Training of TSE Model

Considering that the beginning part of a game might be erratic, we choose to only use time slices from the last 50% time in each match in the first experiment.

---

[4] Manta: https://github.com/dotabuff/manta.

[5] Clarity 2: https://github.com/skadistats/clarity.

[6] Documentation of Steam APIs for DotA2: https://wiki.teamfortress.com/wiki/WebAPI#Dota_2.

[7] Data processing took place in Oct. 2017.

[8] Documentation of OpenDota API for match data: https://docs.opendota.com/#tag/matches.

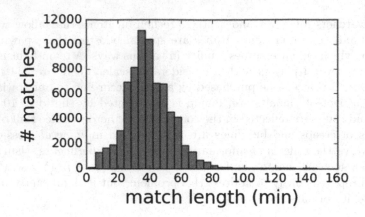

Fig. 4. Distribution of match length

Experiments with whole matches and other range of game time will be talked about in Sect. 3.6. To simplify and get better distribution, we set $r = e - 1$ so $\alpha = 1$. *Adam* optimizer [11] is applied in the experiments.

To better know the optimized hyper-parameters of TSE model, we begin with training and testing partially. We train separately the Ind part with the input described above and y_{scaled} as its output. Each subnet of the Ind part takes in $n_c = 263$ dimensions representing one hero, including 1 for game time, 5 for attributes, 13 for statistics and 244 for items, which is similar to one-tenth of a time slice vector except that hero id is replaced. Due to its structure, only $\frac{c_m}{c_a}$ of the Ind part is trained with every piece of data, so the training process is slower than a fully connected model. For subnets, $l_i = 3, n_i = 40, r_d = 0.5$ are proved to be the best, according to our experiments. We use 90% of the dataset for training, 5% for validation and 5% for testing. This trained Ind part shows an MAE of 0.1523 which indicates a prediction error of 11.15 min.

For the Glo part, we take the time slice vectors directly as input and y_{scaled} as output. $n_m = 400, l_m = 4, r_d = 0.5$ are chosen as the hyper-parameters of the best performance. On the same dataset as the Ind part, the Glo part shows a rescaled MAE of 7.85 min.

For the remaining part of TSE model, $n_c = 4, l_c = 3$ are set. When we train the whole TSE model, we regard it as a multi-output model to avoid training different parts unequally. The loss is calculated by Eq. 13. $\hat{y}_{Ind}$, $\hat{y}_{Glo}$ and $\hat{y}$ are the outputs of Ind part, Glo part, and the whole model.

$$loss = MAE(y, \hat{y}) + \mu \times MAE(y, \hat{y}_{Ind}) + \nu \times MAE(y, \hat{y}_{Glo}) \qquad (13)$$

$\mu = 0.3, \nu = 0.3$ are proved to be an efficient set of parameters in this training. The whole model is trained on the same dataset as previous at first. Then a 10-fold cross validation at match level is applied to provide reliable result.

The result of experiments on partial and full TSE model is shown in Table 1. The performance of TSE model indicates that it is an applicable model to fit

Table 1. Metrics of TSE model

	MAE	MSE	Rescaled MAE (minutes)
Blind prediction	0.5178	0.3683	37.91
Ind part	0.1523	0.0339	11.15
Glo part	0.1072	0.0290	7.85
TSE model	0.1050	0.0287	7.69
TSE model (10-fold cross validation)	0.10539	0.02794	7.716

function DE_{TS}. Both the Ind part and the Glo part are valid compared with blind prediction. The Glo part has a better performance than the Ind part. That means only focusing on the individual contribution separately would result in a significant loss of information. The correlation between heroes plays an essential role in the matches. TSE model combines the two parts and is better than either part, so the validity of both Ind part and Glo part is proven. As TSE model is designed based on the split of individual and global state in MGR analysis, its performance also supports MGR analysis.

3.4 Prediction on Continuous Time Slices

In the previous experiment, time slices are randomly shuffled. We can not discover how TSE model works on continuous time slices from a match. This time we feed time slices generated from a match to the trained TSE model in chronological order and observe its performance on each match. Figure 5 shows the performance of TSE model on four sample test matches. The horizontal axis t represents the remaining time before the end of current match, which declines as the match goes on. The vertical line in the middle splits the graphs into two parts. The right side of it is the last 50% time of the game, which this TSE model is trained to fit.

Focusing on the right side, we can see that TSE model successfully fits DE_{TS} in the last half of matches. It works well on matches of arbitrary lengths no matter Radiant or Dire wins. The predicted value usually fluctuates around the real value. The missing variables such as skills of heroes can be a major reason for such fluctuation.

The observations on whole matches above provide proof of the effectiveness of MOBA-Slice on DotA2. As we can see from the figures, TSE model trained with data of last half matches can evaluate time slices from the last half of new matches thoroughly. This result shows that the functional relationship between the state of a time slice and the game result described in DE_{TS} indeed exists, or TSE model would never be able to work efficiently on new matches. With the figures and the properties of DE_{TS} explained previously, we can see that TSE model can do more than just evaluation. It is also useful enough to work as an online prediction model for the game result and the remaining time.

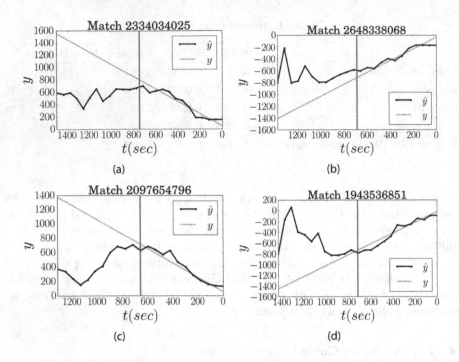

Fig. 5. Performance on sample matches

3.5   Comparison with DotA Plus Assistant on Result Prediction

In the progress of our research, a monthly subscription service called DotA Plus[9] was unveiled in an update of DotA2 on March 12, 2018. As one part of DotA Plus service, Plus Assistant provides a real-time win probability graph for every match, as shown in Fig. 6. It is praised as the "Big Teacher" by Chinese players due to its accurate prediction. Although Plus Assistant can not predict the remaining time of a match, its prediction of game result can be used to evaluate the corresponding ability of MOBA-Slice.

To compare DotA Plus Assistant with MOBA-Slice, we have to choose matches played after its release date, so we can not use the previous dataset. The tournament of DotA2 Asian Championship[10] was held from March 29th to April 7th. This tournament has 105 matches totally, but 33 matches are unusable for network failure or newly introduced heroes that are not included in the training data of our TSE Model. An upsetting fact is that the winning probability data is not available from the replay parser, and is suspected to be encrypted. So we manually download the valid 72 matches in DotA2 client and watch their replay to capture the winning probability graph. We discretize the winning probability into 3 values: Radiant's victory when above the middle line, Dire's when below

---

[9] Homepage of DotA Plus: https://www.dota2.com/plus.
[10] Homepage of DotA2 Asian Championship: http://www.dota2.com.cn/dac/2018/index/?l=english.

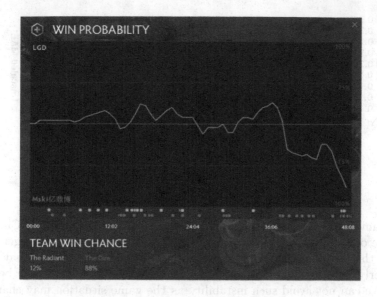

Fig. 6. Win probability graph of DotA plus assistant

it, and unknown when at it. We also feed these matches to the trained TSE model, and discretize the output according to the sign of value as property 1 of DE_{TS} described: positive for Radiant's victory, negative for Dire's, and zero for unknown.

As we have the prediction from both models, we sample the prediction and compare with the real result to calculate the accuracy of a model at a specific game time percent. For example, the prediction results of MOBA-Slice on each match at the time point of 10% of game time are used to calculate the accuracy of MOBA-Slice at 10% time point. The unknown predictions are always counted as errors. We do this calculation every 10% of time for both models, and calculate the average for all time points. As the result in Table 2, the average accuracy of MOBA-Slice is 3.7% higher than DotA Plus Assistant at predicting the game result.

Table 2. Prediction accuracy of MOBA-Slice and DotA Plus Assistant

Game time percent	10%	20%	30 %	40%	50%	60%	70%	80%	90%	Average
DotA Plus Assistant	0.4167	0.5139	0.5972	0.6111	0.6806	0.7500	0.7778	0.8472	0.9444	0.6821
MOBA-Slice	0.5694	0.5417	0.6111	0.7083	0.7083	0.7222	0.8056	0.8611	0.9444	0.7191

3.6 Towards Better Performance

For the first 50% time of the match in Fig. 5, we can see that the error is much larger. One possible reason is that this TSE model is not trained to fit the first

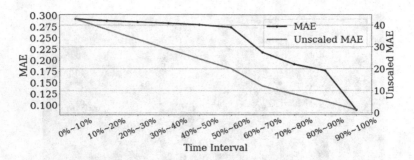

Fig. 7. Experiments on different intervals

half of games, which contains different information from the last half. Changing the range of data is a way to fix this problem. On the other hand, larger insta-bility at the beginning of matches also counts. The game situation may break our underlying assumption for the monotonicity of relative advantage between teams. We can not avoid such instability as the game situation may change at any time. But we can treat this as noise in the data. As long as the instability in training data is relatively small, the models are effective.

We want to see the disparity of instability in different parts of matches, so we train models with time slices from different intervals of game time. As TSE model takes a longer time to train due to the structure of Ind part, we choose to work with merely its Glo part.

As shown in Fig. 7, experiments are carried out for every 10 percent of game time. We train with time slices from 0%–10% of game time and test on 0%–10%, and then repeat training and testing on 10%–20% and so on. The loss decreases as a match goes on, indicating the decline of instability. In other words, it is much more difficult to evaluate the beginning of a match than the ending. In interval 90%–100%, we can predict the game result with an average error of about 1 min, which shows a high relevance of game situation and outcome. But we can not train models specific for an interval of game time to evaluate ongoing matches, as we do not know the length of a match until it ends. We further experiment on larger intervals to find out a proper range of training data for predicting arbitrary time slices.

Results in Fig. 8 are much better than in Fig. 7, since relatively more train-ing data is fed to the model. The same trend that loss decreases as the game progresses is seen in Fig. 8. However, if observed from right to left, Fig. 8 shows something contrary to the common belief that training with more data results in better performance. We find that as time interval gets larger, the model learns from more time slices but the loss keeps growing. The instability of the beginning part seems so large as to worsen the performance. It appears to be a trade-off problem to choose the proper range of training data. The MAE in Fig. 8 cannot be used to determine this as they are calculated on different test sets. We sup-pose the best choice needs to be found in accordance with the performance of MOBA-Slice in actual applications.

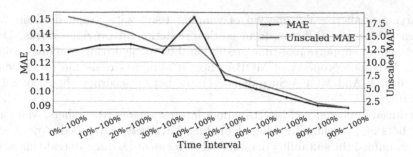

Fig. 8. Experiments on larger intervals

4   Related Work

With the continuously growing number of players, MOBA games have been popular with young people all over the world. As the design of MOBA games is complicated, the large domain of knowledge contained in these games is of great research value. Research related to MOBA games mainly consists three aspects: strategy analysis, result prediction, and AI developing.

Strategy analysis is proved efficient at improving the performance of professional players. Yang and Roberts [25] introduced a data-driven method to do post-competition analysis and knowledge discovery, and evaluated on 3 games: DotA, Warcraft III and Starcraft II. Hao et al. [10] studied player behavior and optimal team positions through clustering. Bauckhage's team [3] introduced a spatio-temporal clustering method to partition game maps into meaningful areas. Cavadenti's group [4] implemented a data mining based method that discovers strategic patterns from historical behavioral traces to help players improve their skills. Hanke and Chaimowicz [9] developed a recommendation system for hero line-ups based on association rules. In most strategy related researches, evaluation of a game situation or the game result is used as a part of the algorithm to tell the effectiveness of a strategy or to optimize toward a bigger winning rate. It is hard for such evaluation to fully utilize the multitudinous variables of MOBA games. In the research of strategy analysis, we also met the problem of evaluation of strategy. This ended up with the proposal of MOBA-Slice. MOBA-Slice is designed to provide reliable quantitative evaluation of game situations. We now suggest using MOBA-Slice as the evaluation algorithm in strategy analysis researches.

It is considered hard to predict the winners of a MOBA game, as the game situation is always changeful. There are so many factors and features to choose from to build a prediction model. Conley and Perry [7] implemented K-Nearest Neighbor (KNN) algorithm to predict with merely hero lineup information. Wang [22] further used multi-layer feedforward neural networks and added game length information into inputs, but did not improve significantly. Almeida's team [1] built classification models of Naive Bayes, KNN, and J48 based on the composition of heroes and the duration of match. Pu et al. [14] also worked towards identifying predictive information of winning team with graph modeling and pattern extraction. Different from static prediction in previous works, DotA Plus Assistant supports real-time prediction, but its algorithm remains business secret. As a nice property of MOBA-Slice, it supports real-time prediction of game results. And MOBA-Slice demonstrates better accuracy than DotA Plus Assistant.

Artificial intelligence of MOBA games interests many researchers. Many rule based bots and machine learning algorithms have been developed. Andersen et al. [2] examined the suitability of online reinforcement learning in real-time strategy games with Tank General as early as 2009. Synnaeve and Bessiere [21] used a semi-supervised method with expectation-maximization algorithm to develop a Bayesian model for opening prediction in RTS games. Kolwankar [12] employed genetic algorithms to adjust actions in evolutionary AI for MOBA. Silva and Chaimowicz [17] implemented a two-layered architecture intelligent agent that handles both navigation and game mechanics for MOBA games. Wisniewski and Miewiadomski [24] developed state search algorithms to provide an intelligent behavior of bots. Pratama et al. [13] designed AI based on fuzzy logic with dynamic difficulty adjustment to avoid static AI mismatching player and AI's difficulty level. AIIDE StarCraft AI competition [6] has been held every year since 2010, with continuously rising popularity. Evaluation of situation is often needed in artificial intelligence algorithms, which MOBA-Slice is designed to provide. MOBA-Slice can work as the reward function in reinforcement learning models [20] and the evaluation function in Monte Carlo planning models [5].

5   Conclusion

MOBA-Slice is a well-designed framework which evaluates relative advantage between teams. It consists three parts: MGR analysis, discounted evaluation, and TSE model. With MGR analysis we manage to describe the deciding factors of MOBA game result. Discounted evaluation function DE_{TS} has several appealing properties one of which is representing the relative advantage between teams. TSE model is designed to fit function DE_{TS}. Through applying MOBA-Slice to DotA2, we prove its effectiveness with experiments on a large number of match replays and comparison with DotA Plus Assistant. MOBA-Slice establishes a foundation for further MOBA related research which requires evaluation methods, including AI developing and strategy analysis.

Here are several aspects listed for future work. The part of the future trend in MGR analysis requires rating algorithm for players and teams. In the experiments, information of heroes' skills and the environment is not taken into consideration due to the current limitation of data processing. More MOBA games can be chosen to apply and test MOBA-Slice. Further, current TSE model is simply based on single time slice. Sequential prediction models can be designed with Recurrent Neural Network to take in time slice sequences, which will provide more information about the game situation.

References

1. Almeida, C.E.M., et al.: Prediction of winners in MOBA games. In: Information Systems and Technologies, pp. 1–6 (2017)
2. Andersen, K.T., Zeng, Y., Christensen, D.D., Tran, D.: Experiments with online reinforcement learning in real-time strategy games. Appl. Artif. Intell. **23**(9), 855–871 (2009)
3. Bauckhage, C., Sifa, R., Drachen, A., Thurau, C.: Beyond heatmaps: spatio-temporal clustering using behavior-based partitioning of game levels. In: Computational Intelligence and Games, pp. 1–8 (2014)
4. Cavadenti, O., Codocedo, V., Boulicaut, J.F., Kaytoue, M.: What did i do wrong in my MOBA game? Mining patterns discriminating deviant behaviours. In: IEEE International Conference on Data Science and Advanced Analytics, pp. 662–671 (2016)
5. Chung, M., Buro, M., Schaeffer, J.: Monte carlo planning in RTS games. In: IEEE Symposium on Computational Intelligence and Games, pp. 117–124 (2005)
6. Churchill, D.: Aiide StarCraft AI competition (2017). http://www.cs.mun.ca/~dchurchill/starcraftaicomp/index.shtml
7. Conley, K., Perry, D.: How does he saw me? A recommendation engine for picking heroes in DotA 2 (2013)
8. Dangauthier, P., Herbrich, R., Minka, T., Graepel, T.: Trueskill through time: revisiting the history of chess. In: International Conference on Neural Information Processing Systems, pp. 337–344 (2007)
9. Hanke, L., Chaimowicz, L.: A recommender system for hero line-ups in MOBA games (2017). https://aaai.org/ocs/index.php/AIIDE/AIIDE17/paper/view/15902/15164
10. Hao, Y.O., Deolalikar, S., Peng, M.: Player behavior and optimal team composition for online multiplayer games. Comput. Sci. 4351–4365 (2015)
11. Kingma, D.P., Ba, J.L.: Adam: a method for stochastic optimization. In: International Conference on Learning Representations (2015)
12. Kolwankar, S.V., Kolwankar, S.V.: Evolutionary artificial intelligence for MOBA/action-RTS games using genetic algorithms, pp. 29–31 (2012)
13. Pratama, N.P.H., Nugroho, S.M.S., Yuniarno, E.M.: Fuzzy controller based AI for dynamic difficulty adjustment for defense of the Ancient 2 (DotA2). In: International Seminar on Intelligent Technology and ITS Applications, pp. 95–100 (2017)
14. Pu, Y., Brent, H., Roberts, D.L.: Identifying patterns in combat that are predictive of success in MOBA games. In: Foundations of Digital Games 2014 Conference (2014)
15. Ramachandran, P., Zoph, B., Le, Q.V.: Searching for activation functions. CoRR abs/1710.05941 (2017). http://arxiv.org/abs/1710.05941
16. Scholkopf, B., Platt, J., Hofmann, T.: TrueSkill: A Bayesian Skill Rating System. MIT Press, Cambridge (2007)
17. Silva, V.D.N., Chaimowicz, L.: On the development of intelligent agents for MOBA games, pp. 142–151 (2016)
18. Silver, D., et al.: Mastering the game of go with deep neural networks and tree search. Nature **529**(7587), 484–489 (2016)
19. Srivastava, N., Hinton, G.E., Krizhevsky, A., Sutskever, I., Salakhutdinov, R.: Dropout: a simple way to prevent neural networks from overfitting. J. Mach. Learn. Res. **15**(1), 1929–1958 (2014)

20. Sutton, R.S., Barto, A.G.: Introduction to Reinforcement Learning, 1st edn. MIT Press, Cambridge (1998)
21. Synnaeve, G., Bessiere, P.: A Bayesian model for opening prediction in RTS games with application to StarCraft. In: Computational Intelligence and Games, pp. 281–288 (2011)
22. Wang, W.: Predicting multiplayer online battle arena (MOBA) game outcome based on hero draft data (2016)
23. Watkins, C.J.C.H., Dayan, P.: Q-learning. Mach. Learn. **8**(3), 279–292 (1992). https://doi.org/10.1007/BF00992698
24. Wiśniewski, M., Niewiadomski, A.: Applying artificial intelligence algorithms in MOBA games. Studia Informatica Syst. Inf. Technol. **1**, 53–64 (2016)
25. Yang, P., Roberts, D.L.: Knowledge discovery for characterizing team success or failure in (A)RTS games. In: Computational Intelligence in Games, pp. 1–8 (2013)

TextWorld: A Learning Environment for Text-Based Games

Marc-Alexandre Côté[1(✉)], Ákos Kádár[2], Xingdi Yuan[1], Ben Kybartas[3], Tavian Barnes[1], Emery Fine[1], James Moore[1], Matthew Hausknecht[1], Layla El Asri[1], Mahmoud Adada[1], Wendy Tay[1], and Adam Trischler[1]

[1] Microsoft Research, Montreal, Canada
macote@microsoft.com
[2] Tilburg University, Tilburg, The Netherlands
[3] McGill University, Montreal, Canada

> The limits of my language mean the limits of my world.
>
> *Ludwig Wittgenstein*

Abstract. We introduce TextWorld, a sandbox learning environment for the training and evaluation of RL agents on text-based games. TextWorld is a Python library that handles interactive play-through of text games, as well as backend functions like state tracking and reward assignment. It comes with a curated list of games whose features and challenges we have analyzed. More significantly, it enables users to hand-craft or automatically generate new games. Its generative mechanisms give precise control over the difficulty, scope, and language of constructed games, and can be used to relax challenges inherent to commercial text games like partial observability and sparse rewards. By generating sets of varied but similar games, TextWorld can also be used to study generalization and transfer learning. We cast text-based games in the Reinforcement Learning formalism, use our framework to develop a set of benchmark games, and evaluate several baseline agents on this set and the curated list.

1 Introduction

Text-based games are complex, interactive simulations in which text describes the game state and players make progress by entering text commands. They are fertile ground for language-focused machine learning research. In addition to language understanding, successful play requires skills like long-term memory and planning, exploration (trial and error), and common sense.

Consider Zork (Infocom 1980), one of the genre's most famous examples. Figure 1 depicts Zork's opening scene along with two player commands and the corresponding system responses. As illustrated, the game uses natural language to describe the state of the world, to accept actions from the player, and to report subsequent changes in the environment. Through sequential decision making,

© Springer Nature Switzerland AG 2019
T. Cazenave et al. (Eds.): CGW 2018, CCIS 1017, pp. 41–75, 2019.
https://doi.org/10.1007/978-3-030-24337-1_3

```
West of House
You are standing in an open field west of a white house, with a boarded
front door.
There is a small mailbox here.

>open mailbox
Opening the small mailbox reveals a leaflet.

>take leaflet
Taken.

>_
```

Fig. 1. Intro to Zork

the player works toward goals which may or may not be specified explicitly. In the nomenclature of reinforcement learning (RL), language is the *action space* and also the *observation space* (Narasimhan et al. 2015). In text-based games, the observation and action spaces are both combinatorial and compositional – major challenges for reinforcement learning. Furthermore, text-based games are partially observable since descriptive text does not communicate complete information about the underlying game state or may do so ambiguously. As a consequence of these (and other) challenges, hand-authored games like Zork are beyond the capabilities of current learning algorithms (Narasimhan et al. 2015; Haroush et al. 2018).

To help agents progress toward mastering text games in a controlled and scientific manner, we introduce the *TextWorld* learning environment. TextWorld is a *sandbox* environment (Wright 1996; Sukhbaatar et al. 2015) in which games of varying complexity emerge from a set of underlying world mechanics. In this setting, simpler games can act as stepping stones toward more complex games. Like the Arcade Learning Environment (ALE, (Bellemare et al. 2013)), Gym (Brockman et al. 2016), and CommAI (Baroni et al. 2017), TextWorld enables interactive play-through of a curated set of games. Unlike previous text-based environments, including TextPlayer and PyFiction, TextWorld's sandbox functionality enables users to handcraft games or to construct games automatically through a suite of generative mechanisms.

Specifically, TextWorld features a logic engine that automatically builds game worlds, populates them with objects and obstacles, and generates quests that define a goal state and how to reach it. It automatically generates text descriptions of underlying game states using an extensible vocabulary and a context-free grammar (CFG). Common-sense rules encoded in the logic and grammar govern generated worlds and the quests within them, to make these human-interpretable and consistent with existing games: *e.g.*, keys open locked doors and can be carried or stored in containers; food items can be combined, cooked, and eaten. Furthermore, because the vocabulary contains synonyms for most nouns, verbs, and adjectives, different surface forms can be applied automatically to abstract types to add variety and complexity: *e.g.*, the `<container>` object may manifest as a *chest* or *cabinet*; the `<move>` action may manifest as `walk` or `go`.

TextWorld's generative nature has several downstream implications for learning. First, it means there exists a known and structured representation of the partially observable game state. This enables exact state-tracking (Henderson et al. 2014) and the corresponding assignment of intermediate rewards in training (if desired). Second, agents can be trained on a potentially infinite set of related text games rather than a finite collection as in previous learning environments. By controlling parameters of the generative process for training and test games, TextWorld can be used to investigate curriculum learning, generalization, and transfer learning in RL. Tunable parameters include the length of quests, the size of environments, the number of abstract action and object types, the number of synonyms for each type, complexity of the descriptive grammar, and more.

A powerful feature of language which motivates our interest in text games is that it abstracts away complex physical processes. For instance, through text an agent could learn and use the concept that *opening doors provides access to connected rooms* without going through the (literal) motions of turning knobs in 3D space and time. This level of abstraction can be useful for studying functions of control, planning, *etc.* in isolation and in tandem with the function of language itself.

The aim of this paper is to introduce TextWorld to the research community. Its primary contributions are:

- A survey of the machine-learning challenges of and approaches to text-based games, including a curated list of hand-authored games with corresponding analysis;
- A detailed description of the TextWorld framework, its features, and how to use it;
- An initial set of simple text games to be used as RL benchmarks;
- Evaluation of several baseline algorithms on both benchmark and hand-authored games.

Subsequent works will more deeply investigate novel approaches to RL for text games. Our hope is that TextWorld becomes a living resource, with contributors developing new benchmarks and algorithms to push the state of the art forward.

The remainder of this paper is organized as follows. In Sect. 2 we introduce text-based games, formalize them as RL problems and highlight their challenges. In Sect. 3 we delve into details of the TextWorld framework, how it generates and interacts with text games, and how it may be used to train RL agents. Section 4 describes related frameworks and existing approaches to solving text games, while Sect. 5 describes some of TextWorld's benchmark tasks and our experimental results. We discuss limitations of the framework and future work in Sect. 6 before concluding.

2   Text Games from a Reinforcement Learning Perspective

Text-based games are sequential decision-making problems that can be described naturally by the Reinforcement Learning (RL) formalism. In this section, we define some of the terminology found in text-based games, formalize the text-based environment as an RL problem, discuss challenges faced by RL agents in such environments, and show how these challenges motivate the need for a framework like TextWorld. In the following, an "agent" is a model that takes text information as input and outputs text commands to progress through a game.

2.1   Text-Based Games

Text-based games are turn-based games usually played through a command line terminal. At each turn, several lines of text describe the state of the game, and the player may enter a text command to change this state in some desirable way (*i.e.*, to move towards a goal). A game's built-in parser or interpreter deciphers player commands and maps them to state changes (events in the game). The genre became popular in the early 1980s especially with the release of Zork (Infocom 1980), which featured rich storytelling and an advanced command parser.

2.1.1   Gameplay

Text-based games can be classified according to how the player issues commands (see Fig. 2): in **parser-based** games, the player types text commands character by character; in **choice-based** games, the player chooses from a given list of command options; and in **hypertext-based** games, the player clicks on one of several links present in the description. The work in this paper focuses on **parser-based** games.

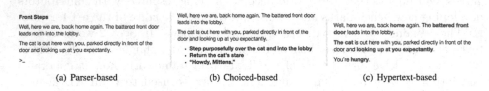

(a) Parser-based   (b) Choiced-based   (c) Hypertext-based

Fig. 2. Types of text-based games. Image from (He et al. 2015).

In text-based game terminology, each discrete in-game location is called a *room* (*e.g.*, "Kitchen", "In front of the white house", and so on). A game may contain one or several rooms connected in some topology forming a *map*. To explore the environment, the player issues navigational commands: go followed by a cardinal direction (*north*, *northeast*, *etc.*) or an orthogonal direction (*up*, *down*). Maps vary greatly from one game to another. Room exits and entrances do not always match (*e.g.*, go north and then go south may not return you to where you started). Also, some navigational commands may not have a reciprocal (*e.g.*, in Zork (Infocom 1980), a trapdoor locks from behind preventing the player from going back).

Most of the time, rooms contain objects the player can interact with (*e.g.*, take sandwich from table, eat sandwich, open door, *etc.*). Objects are defined by their *attributes*, which also determine how the player can interact with them (through object affordances). For instance, an object could be portable (*e.g.*, a lamp) or portable and edible (*e.g.*, a sandwich).

One of the biggest challenges when playing parser-based games is figuring out what are the commands that will be understood by the parser (*i.e.*, that are intended by the game's author). Also, depending on the game, the result of some commands may be stochastic (*e.g.*, go up succeeds 75% of the time, but 25% of the time results in the player falling down to a previous room). A detailed list of puzzles and challenges traditionally found in text-based games can be found in Appendix A.

2.2 Text-Based Games as POMDPs

Fundamentally, text-based games can be seen as partially observable Markov decision processes (POMDP) (Kaelbling et al. 1998) where the environment state is never observed directly. To act optimally, an agent must keep track of all observations, *i.e.*, textual feedback received after entering commands. Although the observation can be augmented with feedback from commands like look and inventory, which describe the agent's surroundings and possessions, this information is still limited to the current room.

Formally, a text-based game is a discrete-time POMDP defined by $(S, T, A, \Omega, O, R, \gamma)$, where S is the set of environment states, T is the set of conditional transition probabilities between states, A is the set of words that are used to compose text commands, Ω is the set of observations, O is a set of conditional observation probabilities, $R : S \times A \to \mathbb{R}$ is the reward function, and $\gamma \in [0, 1]$ is the discount factor.

Environment States (S). The environment state at turn t in the game is $s_t \in S$. It contains the complete internal information of the game, like the position and state of every entity (rooms, objects, player, *etc.*), much of which is hidden from the agent. When an agent issues a command c_t (defined next), the environment transitions to state s_{t+1} with probability $T(s_{t+1}|s_t, c_t)$.

Actions (A). At each turn t, the agent issues a text command c_t of at least one word. In parser-based games, the interpreter can accept any sequence of characters (of any length) but will only recognize a tiny subset thereof. Furthermore, only a fraction of recognized commands will actually change the state of the world. The resulting action space is enormous and intractable for existing RL algorithms. We make the following two simplifying assumptions:

- **Word-level** Commands are sequences of at most L words taken from a fixed vocabulary V.

- **Syntax** Commands have the following structure: verb[noun phrase [adverb phrase]], where [...] indicates that the sub-string is optional. In this context, a noun phrase is a string identifying an object (*e.g.*, "the big wooden chest"). Similarly, an adverb phrase provides additional context for the command (*e.g.*, "with the red key"). To simplify the syntax further, determiners are omitted.[1]

The agent's action space is some vocabulary V plus a special token <return> that indicates the end of a command. Each action $a_t^i \in A$ is a token, where t is the turn in the game and i indicates the ith token in the command c_t. A command is a sequence of $n \le L$ tokens $c_t = [a_t^1, \dots, a_t^n]$ that respects the syntax previously defined and ends with $a_t^n = $ <return>.

The agent's policy is a mapping between its states and actions. In TextWorld, the agent's policy π_θ, where θ are the policy's parameters, maps a state s_t and words generated in the command so far to the next word to generate: $a_t^i = \pi_\theta(s_t, a_t^0, \dots, a_t^{i-1})$.

Observations (Ω). The text information perceived by the agent at a given turn t in the game is the agent's observation, $o_t \in \Omega$, which depends on the environment state and the previous command with probability $O(o_t|s_t, c_{t-1})$. In other words, the function O selects from the environment state what information to show to the agent given the command entered. For instance, if the agent tries to open a chest, the observation returned by the environment might show that the chest is locked.

Reward Function (R). Based on its actions, the agent receives reward signals $r_t = R(s_t, a_t)$. The agent's goal is to maximize the expected discounted sum of rewards received $E\left[\sum_t \gamma^t r_t\right]$.

Most text-based games (including those in our curated list) have a scoring mechanism whereby players receive points for completing (sub)quests and reaching new locations. When available, this score can be used as a reward signal. Otherwise, one could define reward signals by assigning a positive reward if the agent completes the game. Intermediate rewards might also be inferred from the interpreter's feedback. Note that this feedback usually only contains information about the results of individual commands (*e.g.*, "I don't know this verb!", "This chest is locked!") rather than about overall progress.

2.3   RL Challenges in Text-Based Games

Complex environments make training RL agents challenging for several reasons. Here, we list some conventional challenges known in the RL literature that are also prevalent in text-based games.

Partial Observability. As mentioned, states of text-based games are partially observable. Only the local information such as the current room description and the player's inventory is made available. Moreover, taking into account only the

---

[1] Typical text-based game interpreters disregard determiners.

latest observation, it may be impossible to differentiate certain states based on observations. For instance, seeing a blue locked chest in a room, it is important for the agent to know whether or not it collected or saw a blue key in the past. The environment might give the same feedback for two different commands (*e.g.*, "taken" might be the feedback for take blue key or take red apple). Furthermore, important information about the environment might not be apparent in the observation (*e.g.*, whether a chest is locked or not, what it contains, *etc.*). Observations may also be time-sensitive (*e.g.*, the agent only gets a reward when examining clues for the first time).

Large State Space. With large state spaces, tabular methods for solving RL problems are no longer practical (Sutton and Barto 2018). Finding good approximate solutions is still an active area of research. In text-based games, the state space is combinatorial and enormous; the number of possible states increases exponentially with the number of rooms and objects.

Large and Sparse Action Space. As with large state spaces, reasoning in an environment with a large number of actions necessitates finding good approximate solution methods to replace the tabular ones (Sutton and Barto 2018). The text-based game setting is especially challenging since the action space is large and sparse; the space of all word strings is much larger than the space of admissible commands (*i.e.*, commands that actually change the underlying state s_t). In addition, the outcome or even the validity of some commands might depend on a specific event or how much time has passed (*e.g.*, the tide rises and blocks the player in (Bates 1987)).

Exploration vs. Exploitation. Balancing exploration of the environment and the exploitation of known information is a fundamental issue in RL (McFarlane 2003). Exploration is at the core of text-based games as they cannot be solved by learning a purely reactive controller. Instead, a strategy that promotes *directed exploration* must be used; the agent must deliberately explore the environment, collecting information about objects and persons encountered along the way (*e.g.*, you never know what is in a box without opening it first). Such information hints about the goal/purpose of the game, what dangers are present, and provides clues that might become handy later in the game for solving puzzles. We expect that agents, like humans, will benefit from exploration driven by curiosity.

Long-Term Credit Assignment. Knowing which actions were responsible for obtaining a certain reward, especially when rewards are sparse, is another fundamental issue in RL (Sutton and Barto 2018). Sparse rewards are inherent to text-based games in which the agent must generate a sequence of actions before observing a change in the environment state or getting a reward signal. For instance, activating a switch might have no immediate effect although it is essential for completing the game. Most text-based games feature sparse rewards, on the order of a single positive reward every 10–20 steps when following an optimal state trajectory.

2.3.1 Additional Challenges

By their very nature, text-based games bring additional challenges related to natural language understanding.

Observation Modality. Observations consist in the environment's textual feedback to the previous command. This means that the observation space is unbounded, consisting of arbitrary-length sequences of characters. To simplify things, we assume that an observation is made of space-separated words that may or may not be found in an English dictionary. One drawback of looking only at words is that we may lose some information provided by the spacing (*e.g.*, ASCII art in Infidel (Berlyn 1983) or a sonar map in Seastalker (Galley and Lawrence 1984)).

Understanding Parser Feedback. Text-based games process player input using a parser. The parser varies from game to game in terms of the actions it recognizes. For example, nearly all games recognize actions like `get`, `take` and `go`, but only some games recognize verbs like `tickle`, `swim`, `dig` and `bribe`. Part of the challenge of playing a parser-based text game is understanding which verbs and objects are recognized by the parser. Making this task more difficult, failure messages vary from game to game when the parser receives an invalid or unrecognized command.

Common-Sense Reasoning and Affordance Extraction. To succeed at text-based games, it is necessary to understand how to interact with everyday objects. For example, if the description of a location includes a tree, it is likely that a player could climb or chop the tree, but not eat or drive it. The problem of identifying which verbs are applicable to a given object is called *affordance extraction* and learning agents must solve it efficiently to make progress in text-based games without exhaustive search.

Language Acquisition. Some objects and actions may be named with invented words. Also, modifier words affect how some objects can be interacted with (this is related to affordance extraction). The meaning of these words must be learned on-the-fly while interacting with the environment. Text-based games also use linguistic coreference, since it is more pleasant to humans, which can complicate the task for learning machines.

2.4 RL with TextWorld

Solving a single text-based game often corresponds to tackling most of the above challenges at once, which makes it very difficult for existing algorithms. What would be useful is a way of testing and debugging RL agents in simpler settings (*e.g.*, one room with two objects where the goal is to eat the edible one). This is the main purpose of TextWorld's generative functionality (described in Sect. 3.2). It can be used to focus on desired subsets of the challenges listed above.

First, it is possible to control the size of the state space (*e.g.*, the number of rooms, number of objects, and how many commands are required in order to reach the goal optimally). At the moment, TextWorld has deterministic transitions between states.

It is also possible to control the partial observability of the state by augmenting the agent's observations. The environment can provide the agent with a list of objects present in-game or even provide all information about the current game state. For instance, instead of generating the observation that there is a blue chest, the environment could state that the chest is locked and that inside the chest there is a red apple. In this setting, the agent does not need to explore to determine the layout of the world and the objects it contains.

TextWorld enables one to generate a large number of games and control their shared characteristics (map, objects, goals, *etc.*). This is useful for focusing, *e.g.*, on language acquisition and affordance extraction: the agent can be trained on games with a fixed number of rooms and object types but with different object names. By interacting with objects, the agent should learn which have a similar function and generalize from one game instance to another.

There are several ways to ease the language generation task. It is possible to restrict the agent's vocabulary to in-game words only or to restrict the verbs that the agent can generate to those understood by the parser. It is also possible to use a simplified grammar where object names are replaced with symbolic tokens (*e.g.*, "You see container1 and container2."). Language generation can be circumvented completely by converting every generated game into a choice-based game. In this case, commands c_t are the agent's actions, *i.e.*, the agent's output becomes an index into the set of admissible commands (see Sect. 3.3.1) rather a sequence of words.

Finally, instead of earning rewards only at the end of a game if the agent is successful, one can also provide intermediate rewards during training based on environment state transitions and the ground truth winning policy (see Sect. 3.1.1).

3   The TextWorld Learning Environment

TextWorld[2] is a Python framework for training and testing RL agents on text-based games. It enables generation from a game distribution parameterized by the map size, the number of objects, quest length and complexity, richness of text descriptions, and more. The framework's architecture is shown in Fig. 3. We detail the *Engine* component in Sect. 3.1, which covers how the internal state of generated games is represented and how the transition function is defined. The *Generator* component is described in Sect. 3.2, which explains the process of automatic game generation. TextWorld can also be used to play existing text-based games (see a curated list of games in Sect. 5.1) but provides more limited information from the internal states of such games.

---

[2] Code and documentation can be found at http://aka.ms/textworld.

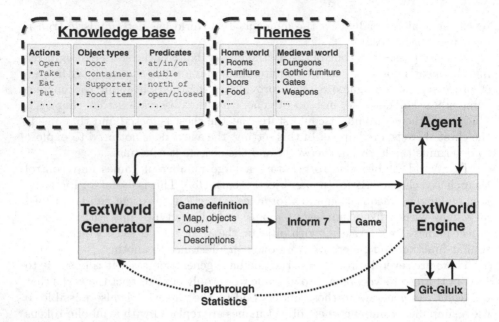

Fig. 3. Overview of the framework. The two main components (in blue) of the proposed pipeline: the game generator and the game engine, which handles interactive play. Inform 7 and Git-Glulx are third-party libraries (in green) and the agent (in red) should be provided by the user. Given some knowledge base, sampled game definitions are first converted to Inform 7 code and compiled into a Glulx executable file. Then, agents interact with the game by communicating with the Git-Glulx interpreter via TextWorld. (Color figure online)

3.1   Game Engine

Game generation in TextWorld relies on a simple inference engine that ensures game validity at every step in the generation process. A game is said to be valid if it is possible to reach the end goal from the initial state. Although we could have used an existing problem-solver for this purpose, we did not require the full power of logical programming languages. TextWorld's inference engine implements simple algorithms specific to our environments, such as a one-step forward and backward chaining with or without fact creation (more on this in Sect. 3.2). In future work our aim is to integrate the TextWorld framework with well established frameworks such as GDL (Genesereth et al. 2005) or STRIPS (Fikes and Nilsson 1971).

To better explain the framework, let's consider the following simple text-based environment. There is a kitchen with a table and a closed fridge in which there is an apple. A visual representation can be seen in Fig. 4. The player is represented by the small avatar and the letter *P*. Objects of the container type are represented by a chest, supporters (or surfaces) are represented by a table

Fig. 4. Simple environment with one room (*kitchen*), a container (*fridge*), a supporter (*table*), a food item (*apple*) and nothing in the player's inventory.

and food-type items are represented by an apple symbol. The anchor symbol next to certain objects means that they are fixed in place (*i.e.*, cannot be taken).

TextWorld's generated text-based games can be represented internally as a Markov Decision Process (MDP) (Puterman 1994) defined by (S, A, T, R, γ), where S is the set of environment states, A is the set of actions (with A_{s_t} those available in state $s_t \in S$), $T(s_t, a, s_{t+1}) = P(s_{t+1}|s_t, a)$ is the state transition function that depends on current state s_t and action taken $a \in A_{s_t}$, $R : S \times A \rightarrow \mathbb{R}$ is the reward function, and $\gamma \in [0, 1]$ is the discount factor. Text-based games are *episodic* since they stop when the player reaches one of the winning (goal) states $G \subset S$.

Note that the MDP part of the POMDP, defined in Sect. 2.2, is semantically equivalent to the one described in this section. The sole exception is the action space; in the POMDP, we assume there exists an underlying function that maps text strings (generated by the agent) to the game actions defined in this section. This is the role of the game's interpreter.

Environment States (S). Game states are defined in terms of logical predicates. Each predicate $\mathbf{p}(v_1, \ldots, v_m)$ consists of a symbol $\mathbf{p}$ drawn from the alphabet of predicates Σ followed by an m-tuple of variables. These *predicates* define the relations between the entities (objects, player, room, *etc.*) present in the game. A *logical atom* is a predicate whose variables are all are bound, *i.e.*, free variables (placeholders) have been substituted by concrete entities.

A game state $s \in S$ consists in a multiset of logical atoms representing the *facts* that are currently true about the world, also known as "resources" in linear logic. Taking as an example Fig. 4, the state depicted there can be represented as

$$s_t = \text{at}(\textit{fridge}, \textit{kitchen}) \otimes \text{at}(\textit{table}, \textit{kitchen}) \otimes \text{in}(\textit{apple}, \textit{fridge})$$
$$\otimes \text{open}(\textit{fridge}) \otimes \text{at}(P, \textit{kitchen}),$$

where the symbol $\otimes$ is the linear logic *multiplicative conjunction* operator.

The set of winning states G is composed of any state s for which all the winning conditions (a set of facts) hold. The winning conditions are determined during the game generation process (Sect. 3.2.2). For instance, a winning condition could be as simple as in($apple, I$), *i.e.*, the apple being in the player's inventory.

State Transition Function (T). The state transition function is defined using linear logic (Russell and Norvig 2016, Chap. 8) and is inspired in part by Ceptre (Martens 2015), a linear logic programming language. Logical rules are stored in a knowledge base and define what is possible in the game. For the working example, the relevant rules are

$$open(C) :: \$at(P, R) \otimes \$at(C, R) \otimes closed(C) \multimap open(C)$$
$$close(C) :: \$at(P, R) \otimes \$at(C, R) \otimes open(C) \multimap closed(C)$$
$$take(F, C) :: \$at(P, R) \otimes \$at(C, R) \otimes \$open(C) \otimes in(F, C) \multimap in(F, I)$$
$$take(F, S) :: \$at(P, R) \otimes \$at(S, R) \otimes on(F, S) \multimap in(F, I)$$
$$put(F, S) :: \$at(P, R) \otimes \$at(C, R) \otimes \$open(C) \otimes in(F, I) \multimap in(F, C)$$
$$insert(F, C) :: \$at(P, R) \otimes \$at(S, R) \otimes in(F, I) \multimap on(F, S)$$
$$eat(F, S) :: in(F, I) \multimap eaten(F).$$

The uppercase italic letters represent variables for objects of a certain type (F: food item, S: supporter, C: container and R: room). The entities P and I represent the player and its inventory. The symbol $\multimap$ (lolli) is the linear implication operator. The interpretation of the linear implication is such that it *consumes* the resources on the *left-hand-side* (henceforth LHS) and *generates* resources on the *right-hand-side* (henceforth RHS). The notation $ is a shorthand meaning a predicate is implicitly carried over to the right-hand side. Given a state and the set of rules, we can perform *forward chaining*. Applying a rule to state s, whose LHS is satisfied by s, leads to a conclusion, which is a new collection of atoms generated by the RHS of the selected rule.

Applying all possible rules for all conclusions leads to a proof-tree with triplets (s, a, s'), where s is an assumption and rule a leads to the conclusion s'. Adding control to forward chaining, by only exploring paths where unseen states are introduced, leads to an algorithm that upon termination discovers all $s \in S$ in the MDP. Merging the duplicate states in the proof-tree provides the underlying (S, A, T) of the MDP.

Action Space (A). An action is one of the rules defined in the knowledge base for which all free variables have been "grounded", *i.e.*, substituted by bound variables appropriately. Actions available in the current state, A_{s_t}, can be obtained by performing a single step of forward-chaining given facts true in s_t. In other words, the inference engine is used to retrieve all possible substitutions for every rule that can be applied to s_t. In the initial state of the working example, the available actions are

$close(fridge) ::$

$\quad \$\text{at}(P, kitchen) \otimes \$\text{at}(fridge, kitchen) \otimes \text{open}(fridge) \multimap \text{closed}(fridge)$

$take(apple, fridge) ::$

$\quad \$\text{at}(P, kitchen) \otimes \$\text{at}(fridge, kitchen)$

$\quad \otimes \$\text{open}(fridge) \otimes \text{in}(apple, fridge) \multimap \text{in}(apple, I)$

Reward Function (R). In the general case, games generated with TextWorld only provide a positive reward when reaching a winning state $s \in G$. The goal is to maximize the expected discounted sum of rewards received $E\left[\sum_t \gamma^t r_t\right]$ where $r_t = R(s_t, a_t)$.

3.1.1   Intermediate Reward

Tracking the state of the player allows us to determine a winning policy (not necessarily optimal) for any game state. A prerequisite is that a winning policy exists from the player's initial position (this is guaranteed for generated games). If so, then by monitoring state changes we can update the winning policy accordingly: if the agent performs the action dictated by the current winning policy, it progresses to the next desired state and we simply shift the policy forward one time-step; if the agent goes off the winning trajectory we add reciprocal actions to the policy to undo or correct this negative progress; and if the agent changes its state in a way that does not affect the quest, the winning policy does not change.

In addition to the final reward, TextWorld can provide an intermediate reward which is tied to the winning policy. After each command, if the winning policy increases in length, meaning that as a result of the last action, additional commands are required to solve the game, then we assign a negative reward. If the winning policy shortens, meaning the last action brought the agent closer to the goal, we assign a positive reward. Otherwise, the reward is 0.

3.2   Game Generation

TextWorld can be used as a sandbox environment in which predefined dynamics govern emergent games. With this sandbox, it is possible to generate a combinatorial (not to say infinite) set of games from which an agent could learn the underlying dynamics. Since we control the generation process, we can construct games where the knowledge to be learned is interpretable to humans.

TextWorld's game generator takes as input a high-level specification of a game and outputs the corresponding executable game source code in the Inform 7 language (Appendix C). The game specification assigns values to parameters such as the number of rooms, the number of objects, the length of the quest, the winning conditions, and options for the text generation (*e.g.*, theme, co-references, adjectives, and so on).

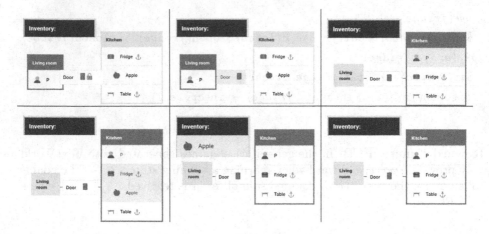

Fig. 5. Comic strip showing a simple quest where the player has to find and eat the apple.

3.2.1 World Generation

TextWorld generates maps through a simple procedure based on the Random Walk algorithm (Pearson 1905). This enables us to generate a wide variety of room configurations, which in turn makes the set of possible games very large. The map generation process is parameterized by the number of rooms, the grid size of the world, and whether room connections should have doors or not. The grid size influences the compactness of the room configuration, where smaller grids mean more compact maps with potentially more loops.

Once the map is generated, objects are added to the world uniformly across the rooms. Some objects are `portable` (as opposed to `fixed in place`), which means they can be nested on or in other objects that have the `supporter` or `container` attribute, or placed on the floor of a room or in the player's inventory.

3.2.2 Quest Generation

In TextWorld, the purpose of any game is to reach a winning state. The term *quest* will be used to represent a sequence of actions the player must perform to win the game. Note that this sequence does not have to be optimal or unique; many trajectories could lead to a winning state.

We define *quest generation* as the process of determining interesting sequences of actions from which to derive winning conditions. As discussed in Sect. 3.1, the inference engine in TextWord can perform forward-chaining to construct a tree of all possible action sequences given an environment. However, not all paths are interesting (from a human or RL perspective). For this reason, we impose a dependency constraint on the actions and reject paths containing cycles. The dependency relation is defined as follows: action a_t depends on action a_{t-1} if and only if the RHS of a_{t-1} generates the resource(s) required by the LHS

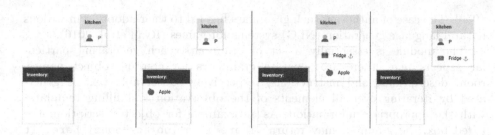

Fig. 6. Comic strip showing backward quest generation for the quest `open fridge` / `take apple from fridge` / `eat apple`. The player is first placed in the kitchen. The apple is created and placed in the player's inventory at Step 2. The fridge is created at Step 3, and the apple placed within it. In the last step the fridge is closed. This becomes the game's starting state.

of a_t. The winning condition of a given quest is the set of resources generated by the RHS of the last action.

We can generate quests by modifying the forward chaining algorithm to apply these constraints, calling the resulting process *forward quest generation*. An example quest is depicted in Fig. 5. First, the player opens the door and moves south to enter the kitchen. When in the kitchen, the player opens the fridge, takes the apple, and finally eats it.

Backward Quest Generation. The end goal often defines the nature of a quest and yields significant rewards for the agent. Thus, it is desirable to specify the end goal in quest generation. The forward quest generation algorithm indirectly allows this specification, by generating all possible quests from an initial condition then searching for those that satisfy the ending constraint. However, as the number of states and the length of the desired quest increases, this approach becomes intractable. To remedy this, TextWorld also supports backward chaining. Backward chaining simply reverses forward chaining, starting from a specified end state rather than an initial state. The same dependency between subsequent actions and cycle rejection apply.

Extending the World during Quest Generation. TextWorld's generator extends forward and backward chaining with a *fact creation* step, which may occur before sampling a subsequent (or previous) action. Through fact creation, the generative process can add missing objects and facts to the world as needed, which yields more diverse quests and games. Figure 6 shows a simple example of backward quest generation.

3.2.3 Text Generation
The Text Generation module takes logical elements of the game state and renders them into coherent text. This serves as the observation provided to the agent. The engine generates object names, room descriptions, and quest instructions in constrained natural language using a context-free grammar (CFG) (Chomsky

1956). The ease of authoring such grammars has led to their adoption in various natural language generation (NLG) systems for games (Ryan et al. 2016).

The module is essentially a set of grammars, each generating particular aspects: *e.g.*, there are separate grammars for creating object names, room descriptions, and instructions, respectively. Observable text is generated by iterating over all elements of the observation and filling templates with the appropriate information. As an example for object description: For a red box, the grammar may return "There is a [object-noun] here. It is [object-adjective]"., which is filled to create "There is a box here. It is red." Some basic maintenance also ensures fluency, *e.g.*, using "an" vs. "a" when a noun begins with a vowel.

Using a context-free grammar gives a degree of textual variation, allowing the same world and quest to be represented a number of ways while also ensuring strict control over the results. While our current grammars function like a text templating system, CFGs offer the possibility of deeper, recursive text generation should it be desired. Our grammars can be extended and modified easily with additional production rules, enabling the generation of simpler or more complex sentence structures that may act as a level of game difficulty.

Object Names. Object names are assigned to each term in the game. Names are randomly picked from the CFG and uniquely assigned to objects. The object's type is used to derive the start symbol sent to query the CFG for a name. An object name can be decomposed into two parts: adjective and noun. The adjective is optional, and may be used to create more complex object names, and correspondingly more complex descriptions. Object name generation is in general straightforward, and consists of selecting a random adjective and noun and combining them. So, *e.g.*, given the nouns "box" and "cup", as well as the adjectives "dusty" and "red", there are four possible object names, "dusty box", "red box", "dusty cup" and "red cup". Adjectives are also used as hints to the player; for example, a key's adjective will always match the adjective of what it opens, *e.g.*, a "red key" will open the "red chest".

Room Descriptions. The description of a room is the concatenation of the *room-level* description of every object it contains, shown typically when entering the room or upon using the look command. The room-level description of an object contains information the player should be aware of upon entering the room (*e.g.*, "There is a chest here. It is open and you can see some gold coins in it."). The room's description also mentions its possible exits (*e.g.*, "There is a path leading north."). It is updated dynamically based on changes to the states of objects in the room, for example listing whether a container is open, closed, or locked, and which objects it contains.

Quest Instructions. We use instructions to explain to the player what to do in a game. An instruction is a piece of text describing a particular action or several different actions. For example, "Retrieve the blue key" could be used to represent the action take blue key, whereas "Take the red key from the locked chest" may represent the sequence of actions unlock chest / open chest

```
Your objective is to sit the tiny grape on the dusty bench i
n the luxurious steam room.

-= Unreasonably Hot Dish-Pit =-
This might come as a shock to you, but you've just moved int
o an unreasonably hot dish-pit. You begin looking for stuff.

A locked safe is here. You can make out a soaped down saucep
an. You see a yellow passkey on the saucepan. I mean, just w
ow! Isn't TextWorld just the best?

There is an exit to the south. Don't worry, it is unblocked.

There is a chilled sandwich on the floor.

> take sandwich
Taken.

> inventory
You are carrying:
  a chilled sandwich
  a large stick of butter

> eat it
You eat the chilled sandwich. Not bad.

>  _
```

```
The objective is to put adj9 snack3 on adj44 stand0.

-= Adj99 Room99 =-
You are in the adj99 room99.

There is a closed C-box here. There is an adj44 stand9 here.
The adj44 stand9 holds a C-key.

There is an exit to the south.

There is an adj6 snack6 on the floor.

> take snack6
Taken.

> inventory
You are carrying:
  an adj6 snack6
  an adj46 snack66

> eat it
You eat the adj6 snack6. Not bad.

>  _
```

(a) House   (b) Basic

Fig. 7. The same generated game with two themed grammars: house and basic.

/ `take red key`. In TextWorld, instructions may optionally describe every action of a quest (easier), only the final action (harder), or they may force the player to figure out what to do from scratch (goal identification; hardest). Likewise, the ability to combine actions into a single instruction can also be toggled; identifying a sequence of actions from an instruction rather than a single action is an additional challenge.

Text Generation Options. TextWorld offers some control over different aspects of the text generation. Objects with similar attributes/states can be grouped together when describing a room (*e.g.*, "In here, you see two red containers: a box and a chest."). Objects mentioned in an instruction can be referred to using one or several of their attributes (*e.g.*, "Take the red edible thing."). Use of coreference (*e.g.*, "There is a chest. It is open. In it, you see nothing interesting.") is also optional.

TextWorld also offers the choice between two themed grammars: house and basic. The house theme describes the world as if the game takes place in a modern house. The second theme uses a simple grammar with almost no linguistic variation (*e.g.*, no adjectives, no multi-word names). In this case, objects with the same attributes use a shared, prototypical prefix for their names followed by a number (*e.g.*, *stand42*). The basic grammar cuts down the vocabulary and the language complexity to ease the training of neural generative models. These house and basic themes can be seen applied to the same underlying game in Fig. 7 (Fig. 8).

3.3   Game Interaction with TextWorld

Most basically, TextWorld can be used to play any text-based games that are interpretable either by Z-machine (via the Frotz interpreter) or by Glulx (via a custom git-glulx interpreter). The framework handles launching and interacting with the necessary game processes. It provides a simple API for game interaction

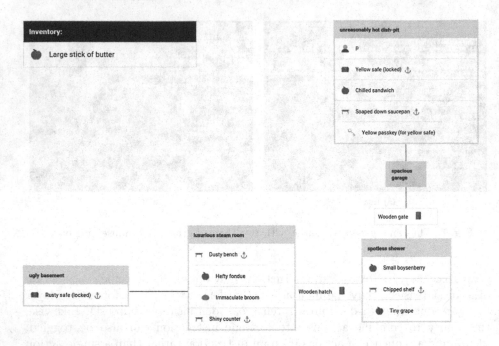

Fig. 8. Visualization of the game shown in Fig. 7 using TextWorld's integrated game-state viewer. The winning sequence of commands for this game: go south / go south / take tiny grape from chipped shelf / go west / put tiny grape on dusty bench.

inspired by that of OpenAI's Gym (Brockman et al. 2016). As an example, playing a text-based game requires just a few lines of Python code:

```
import textworld
env = textworld.start("zork1.z5")
game_state = env.reset()   # Reset/initialize the game.
reward, done = 0, False
while not done:
    # Ask the agent for a command.
    command = agent.act(game_state, reward, done)
    # Send the command to the game and get the new state.
    game_state, reward, done = env.step(command)
```

3.3.1 Game Observation

The game_state object contains useful information[3] such as:

Feedback. The interpreter's response to the previous command, *i.e.*, any text displayed on screen.

---

[3] See the framework's documentation for a list of all information obtainable from the game state object.

Description. The description of the current room, *i.e.*, the output of the `look` command.

Inventory. The player's inventory, *i.e.*, the output of the `inventory` command.

Location. The name of the current room.

Score. The current score.

Game state information is fairly limited when it comes to existing games, whereas games generated with TextWorld can provide much more information if desired. Additional information includes:

Objective. Text describing what the player must do to win the game.

Admissible Commands. A list of commands that are guaranteed (i) to be understood by the interpreter and (ii) to affect the game state or to return information of the game state. Using this information in any way corresponds to playing a *choice-based* game rather than a parser-based one.

Intermediate Reward. A numerical value representing how useful the last command was for solving the game (as described in Sect. 3.1.1).

Winning Policy. A list of commands that guarantees winning the game starting from the current game state.

4 Related Work

Text-based games are hard to solve, even for humans, because they require language understanding, planning, and efficient exploration to a greater degree than perception and reflexes (like most Atari games). Nonetheless, a few researchers have tried different approaches that we report in Sect. 4.1. Since TextWorld is a new learning environment, we compare it to relevant frameworks in Sect. 4.2.

4.1 Relevant Models

Narasimhan et al. (2015) develop a two-stage model called LSTM-DQN for parser-based text games, using the deep Q-learning framework. Their model encodes the agent's observation o (a sequence of words) using mean-pooled LSTM states. The resulting state representation is used by two sub-networks to predict the Q-value over all verbs w_v and object words w_o independently. The average of the 2 resulting scores gives the Q-values for the composed actions.

$$Q(s, (w_v, w_o)) = \frac{Q(s, w_o) + Q(s, w_v)}{2} \tag{1}$$

$$Q(s, w_o) = MLP_o(s), \; Q(s, w_v) = MLP_v(s) \tag{2}$$

$$s = LSTM(o), \text{ where } o = w_1 \ldots w_n \tag{3}$$

They test their approach on 2 environments – Homeworld and Fantasyworld – using the Evennia toolkit[4]. Homeworld is a small environment with 4 rooms, a

---

[4] http://www.evennia.com/.

vocabulary of 84 words, and 4 quests. Quests are also specified through text; for example, "Not you are sleepy now but you are hungry now" (which indicates that the player should obtain food but should not get into bed). Fantasyworld is much larger, with a vocabulary size of 1340, and has stochastic state transitions. The LSTM-DQN completes 100% of the quests in Homeworld and 96% of quests in Fantasyworld. The authors also perform transfer-learning experiments by defining Homeworld2, which is made by shuffling the rooms and paths from Homeworld. The LSTM-DQN is trained on Homeworld and the LSTM component is transferred to Homeworld2. The transferred agent learns faster than one without training on Homeworld.

He et al. (2015) introduce the Deep Reinforcement Relevance Network (DRRN) for tackling choice-based text games. They evaluate the DRRN on a deterministic game called "Saving John" and a larger-scale stochastic game called "Machine of Death". These games have vocabulary sizes 1762 and 2258 and action vocabulary sizes of 171 and 419, respectively. The DRRN takes as input the observation o of the state s and action choices a_j and computes a Q-value for each possible pair:

$$Q(s, a_j) = g(f_s(o), f_a(a_j)), \text{ where } o = w_1 \dots w_n \tag{4}$$

The DRRN model converges on both games when trained with the DQN algorithm with experience replay and Boltzmann exploration. It achieves optimal cumulative-reward on Saving John and a suboptimal but stable policy on Machine of Death. The authors test the DRRN trained on Machine of Death on state-action pairs paraphrased by participants. They show high correlation between the original and paraphrase $Q(s, a, \theta)$.

Note that neither the LSTM-DQN nor the DRRN conditions on previous actions or observations. This means that neither has the capacity to deal with partial observability.

Related work has been done to reduce the action space for parser-based games. Haroush et al. (2018) introduce the Action Elimination Network to estimate the probability of an action failing in a given scene. To achieve this, feedback from the game engine is also stored in the replay buffer in addition to the standard <observation, action, reward> triplets. The elimination module is trained with the stored quadruplets and assigns a score to each element in the large set of actions. During ϵ-greedy exploration, at the greedy step the agent is only allowed to consider the top-k actions, while during exploration, random actions are rejected with a predefined probability if their score is below a threshold.

Fulda et al. (2017) tried to accomplish something similar by training word embeddings to be aware of verb-noun affordances. From that embedding, they manually select a group of verb-noun pairs for which they assume the vector $emb(noun) - emb(verb)$ encodes the affordance relation. Using the average of such vectors gives them an "affordance vector" that can be used to project the embedding of new nouns to a region of the embedding space where relevant verbs should be found.

Kostka et al. (2017) build an agent specifically targeting the domain of classic text-based games. They pre-train an LSTM language model on fantasy books that is used in their model to extract important keywords from scene descriptions. Furthermore, they collect a list of possible commands from game solutions and semi-automatically extract a large number of commands from online tutorials and decompiled game sources. Their system follows a modular design where each typical phase of text-adventure gameplay is modeled by a separate algorithm: command generation, battle mode, inventory management, exploration, restart. Their model generates commands by finding keywords in the scene text and cross-referencing the extracted command corpus to find plausible commands.

4.2 Frameworks

In the fields of AI in general and RL in particular, games have played a major role in advancing the state of the art. The well-known Arcade Learning Environment (ALE) (Bellemare et al. 2013), which provides an interface to Atari 2600 games, led to human-level videogame play by deep RL algorithms (Mnih et al. 2015). One limitation of ALE, however, is that it does not facilitate research in generalization, metalearning, and transfer learning because the individual games are too distinct from one other. Indeed, most research using ALE focuses on training a separate agent (with the same architecture) for each game (Machado et al. 2017).

ALE-style game collections exist in contrast to *sandbox* environments, in which games emerge from a set of underlying world mechanics. Perhaps the best known such environment is SimCity (Wright 1996). Sandboxes generate a series of games that share components, and thereby naturally overcome some limitations of collections. Sandbox environments also allow for the programmatic construction of game variants whose difficulty can be tuned to form a curriculum.

The MazeBase environment (Sukhbaatar et al. 2015), possibly the sandbox framework most similar to TextWorld, enables researchers to generate two-dimensional grid-based games. Each grid point may contain a certain object type, such as an obstacle, a pushable block, a switch, or the goal. Maps are provided in an egocentric text-based representation to the player. One of the main motivations of MazeBase is to foster research in learning algorithms that reuse knowledge and policies acquired in related environments and games. Quests and the language in TextWorld are significantly more complex than in MazeBase.

The CommAI framework (Baroni et al. 2017) emphasizes the ability to generate curricula (Bengio et al. 2009), so that agents may learn incrementally from environments of increasing complexity. Interaction with the environment takes place at the lower level of bits rather than simplified natural language as in TextWorld.

Recently, multimodal visuo-linguistic environments were introduced to study grounded language learning through RL. Chaplot et al. (2017) customized the VizDoom platform (Kempka et al. 2016) for language grounding experiments: objects with certain properties are placed in a room and the agent is instrcuted which object(s) to find. To perform similar experiments, Hermann et al. (2017)

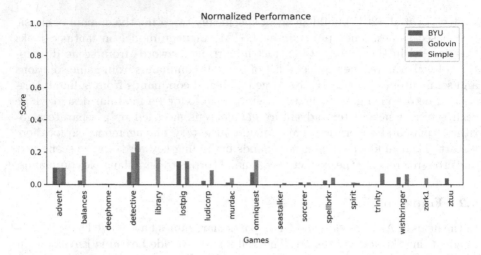

Fig. 9. Normalized score for baselines evaluated on the curated list. Games where no score was obtained are omitted.

add a language instruction component to the DeepMind Lab 3D navigation environment (Beattie et al. 2016).

5   Benchmarks

In this section, we describe benchmark games that can be used through TextWorld to evaluate RL agents and algorithms. This set is preliminary; we plan to develop increasingly complex benchmarks in future work.

5.1   Curated List

Following Fulda et al. (2017), we compiled a list of 50 hand-authored text games to use as an evaluation set. Games designed for human players require, and can be used to measure, general capabilities like common-sense reasoning, planning, and language understanding. We manually analyzed all games in the set to ensure they are valid, with scores and interesting quests. From the original 50 proposed by Fulda et al. (2017), we replaced 20 which were either parodies of text-based games or did not provide scores. The information we collected for the games can be found in Appendix B.

We evaluate three baselines on the proposed list. BYU[5] and Golovin[6] are agents developed by Fulda et al. (2017) and Kostka et al. (2017), respectively, and are described in Sect. 4.1. Both models were submitted to the Text-Based Adventure AI Competition (Atkinson et al. 2018) which consisted in playing

---

[5] Implementation from https://github.com/danielricks/BYU-Agent-2016.
[6] Implementation from https://github.com/Kostero/text_rpg_ai.

20 hidden games. The third is the *Simple* baseline, which consists in sampling uniformly a command from a predefined set[7] at every step.

Each agent has 1000 steps to get a high score. If the agent loses the game, the game is reset and play resumes until the step limit is reached. If the agent wins (which never happens in practice), the game stops and the evaluation is done. The procedure proposed here is slightly different from that in Fulda et al. (2017), where they allow agents to play each game 1000 times for a maximum of 1000 steps each (*i.e.*, a theoretical limit of a million interactions). Our main motivation for having a small "time" budget is that we are interested in measuring the generalization capabilities of agents. When using this evaluation, we assume the agents are already trained (on other similar games) or encompass some prior knowledge (which is the case for the three baselines).

Figure 9 reports the normalized score (*i.e.*, maximum score achieved divided by the game's max possible score) for each baseline agent on the curated list. Unsurprisingly, agents achieve a rather low score on a few games and zero on many. Using the information we gathered during our analysis, we can make educated guesses as to why some baselines perform well on certain games. For instance, in Advent the player starts with 36 points, which explains why all three baselines have the same score. As another example, the Detective game can be solved with mostly navigational commands. This explains why the Simple agent performs relatively well, since the commands it samples from are mostly navigational.

5.2   Treasure Hunter

This benchmark is inspired by the task proposed in Parisotto and Salakhutdinov (2017), where the agent spawns in a randomly generated maze and must find a specific object. A colored "indicator" object near the agent's starting position determines which object the agent must retrieve. The agent earns a positive reward for retrieving the correct object or a negative reward for an incorrect object. There is a limited number of turns.

We adapted this task, which takes place in a 3D environment, to TextWorld. In our setting, the maze is a randomly generated map (see Sect. 3.2.1) of rooms. We randomly place the agent and two objects on the map. Then, we randomly select which object the agent should recover and mention it in the welcome message (our indicator). In navigating to and obtaining the desired object, the agent may have to complete other tasks like finding keys and unlocking doors.

The aim of this benchmark is to assess skills of affordance extraction (agents should determine verb-noun pairs that change the environment state); efficient navigation (agents should avoid revisiting irrelevant rooms); and memory(agents should remember which object to retrieve).

---

[7] The exact set is: north, south, east, west, up, down, look, inventory, take all, drop and YES.

We define the difficulty levels for this benchmark as follows:

- **1 to 10:** Mode: easy, #rooms = 5, quest length linearly increasing from 1 to 5;
- **11 to 20:** Mode: medium, #rooms = 10, quest length linearly increasing from 2 to 10;
- **21 to 30:** Mode: hard, #rooms = 20, quest length linearly increasing from 3 to 20;

where the modes are defined as

- **Easy:** Rooms are all empty except where the two objects are placed. Also, connections between rooms have no door;
- **Medium:** Rooms may be connected by closed doors. Container objects are added, and might need to be opened to find the object;
- **Hard:** Locked doors and containers are added which may need to be unlocked (and opened) to reach the object.

Note that beyond the predefined difficulty levels, this benchmark can be simplified by letting the agent directly tap into the game state information (*e.g.*, feedback, description, inventory and objective) or using a simpler grammar.

5.2.1   Evaluation: One-Life Game

One of our desiderata in building TextWorld is the ability to generate unseen games, so that we can train and evaluate an agent's performance on different game sets. To support our claim of this need, we test two state-of-the-art agents on a set of games generated by TextWorld, where the agents only see each game once and therefore cannot memorize them.

Specifically, for each difficulty level described above, we generate 100 games. We run each agent on these games for a maximum of 1000 steps. For each game, when the agent picks up either the right object or the wrong one, it receives +1 or −1 score, respectively, and the game terminates immediately; if the agent exhausts all 1000 steps without finding any object, it receives 0 score.

Evaluation results are provided in Table 1, where we compare a choice-based[8] random agent (*i.e.*, at each game-step the baseline model randomly selects one command from the list of admissible commands), the BYU agent and the Golovin agent. We report the average score for different difficulty levels and the average number of steps it took to finish the games (either win, lose, or exhaust).

---

[8] Because of the compositional properties of language, a random parser-based agent would perform poorly since most generated commands would not make sense. In this work we use a choice-based random agent. It is not directly comparable to the other two agents, but it can give a general idea how difficult the games are in different difficulty levels.

Table 1. Model performance on one-life treasure hunter tasks.

Model	Random		BYU		Golovin	
	Avg. score	Avg. steps	Avg. score	Avg. steps	Avg. score	Avg. steps
level 1	0.35	9.85	0.75	85.18	**0.78**	18.16
level 5	**−0.16**	19.43	−0.33	988.72	−0.35	135.67
level 10	−0.14	20.74	**−0.04**	1000	−0.05	609.16
level 11	**0.30**	43.75	0.02	992.10	0.04	830.45
level 15	**0.27**	63.78	0.01	998	0.03	874.32
level 20	**0.21**	74.80	0.02	962.27	0.04	907.67
level 21	**0.39**	91.15	0.04	952.78	0.09	928.83
level 25	**0.26**	101.67	0.00	974.14	0.04	931.57
level 30	**0.26**	108.38	0.04	927.37	0.04	918.88

6 Current Limitations

Complex Quest Generation. We define a quest as a sequence of actions where each action depends of the outcomes of its predecessor (Sect. 3.2.2). This limits us to simple quests where each action is based on only the immediately previous action. Quests are rarely so straightforward in text adventure games, often being composed of multiple sub-quests. One method for generating more complex quests would be by treating a quest as a directed graph of dependent actions rather than a linear chain.

Time-Based Events. In the current implementation, there is no support for triggering state changes without corresponding user actions. This would enable doors that automatically lock after a certain number of player steps or traps that trigger periodically (Fig. 10).

Non-Player Characters (NPCs). NPCs are characters that are not controlled by the player and are capable of performing autonomous or reactive actions that alter the game state. NPC interaction is quite common in several text-based games, but is not currently supported by the game generator.

Multi-User Dungeon(MUD). Some text-based games allow multiple users to interact with the world at the same time. Users may need to cooperate with each other or to compete against each other, depending on the game. The framework currently supports only single-agent games.

Text Generation. Using a CFG for text generation makes it difficult to ensure continuity between sentences.

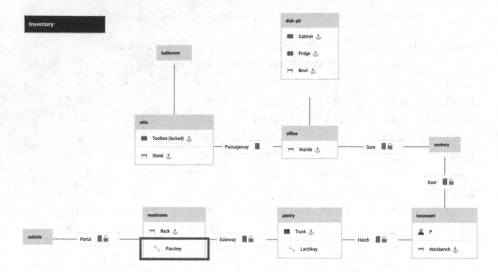

Fig. 10. A generated Treasure Hunter game with difficulty 20. The green rectangle identifies the quest object, a *passkey*, which can be found on a *rack* in the *washroom*. The player, *P*, is currently two rooms away in the *basement* separated by two closed doors. (Color figure online)

7 Conclusion

We introduced TextWorld, a sandbox learning environment for the training and evaluation of RL agents on text-based games. After surveying the machine-learning challenges of text-based games, we cast them in the formalism of reinforcement learning. We described how the generative mechanisms of TextWorld can be used to work up towards the full complexity of hand-authored games and introduced a preliminary set of benchmark games for this purpose. We evaluated several baseline agents on this set and a curated list of hand-authored games that we analyzed.

In future work, we will develop more complex benchmark tasks and investigate novel approaches to representation learning, language understanding and generation, and RL for text-based games.

Acknowledgement. We thank Adam Ferguson and Marion Zepf for many helpful discussions on game analysis. We thank Alessandro Sordoni, Greg Yang, Philip Bachman, Ricky Loynd, Samira Ebrahimi Kahou, and Yoshua Bengio for helpful suggestions and comments on research perspectives. We also thank Ruo Yu Tao for his help with the visualization.

A   Typical Text-Based Obstacles

Language. Language presents a number of difficulties Parser complexity (what a parser can and cannot handle), distracting in-game descriptions, sarcasm (e.g., If the game responds "`Yeah right, that's totally going to work`" when you enter a command, a solid understanding of sarcasm would prevent you from repeating the command), and fictional languages.

Maze. One of the oldest text adventure obstacles, the most basic maze is a grid of rooms with similar names and/or descriptions. The player has to find the right path through the maze to reach a goal. Many text-based games take care to innovate/complicate mazes. Some innovations include:

- Mazes whose solution is determined stochastically, either on a play-through by play-through basis or on a turn by turn basis.
- Mazes whose configuration changes due to a player action, as in Zork III (Infocom 1982), where the player can move some walls in the maze in order to solve it.
- Mazes that are not solvable by navigation: In Photopia, for example, the player is wearing a spacesuit while navigating the maze. If the player removes the suit, it is revealed that the player has a pair of wings. The player is then able to fly over the maze.

Clue Hunting. Detective games require the player to hunt for clues that will tell them where to go next. In Sherlock, the game begins when the player receives a coded poem that directs them to Westminster Abbey, where they have to solve a number of riddle puzzles in order to find out where to find five different gems, each of which provides the player with further clues. A point of interest here is whether or not the player actually needs to get the hints in order to win the game, or whether the player could win the game if they already knew the contents of the hints. Sherlock (Bates 1987) is an example of the former – some hints trigger crucial game state changes only once the player examines them. Other games mix state-changing hints with purely informative ones. For example, in Inhumane (Plotkin 1985), a clue gives you directions through a maze which is still solvable if you don't find the clue. However, the end of the maze yields another clue. When you read this second clue, an important portion of the map becomes available to the player.

Treasure Hunting. Some treasures double as clues (as is the case with the gems in Sherlock) while other treasures are necessary in order to unlock further treasures. In Infidel, for example, you are given the opportunity to take some gem clusters early in the game. Towards the end of the game, these clusters are used to unlock a treasure chest. (Berlyn 1983).

Trivia. Many games base their puzzles off of trivia/world knowledge, which the player might need to know in order to solve a puzzle. Many puzzles in the Hitchhiker's Guide to the Galaxy game are easier to solve if you are familiar with the source material. For example, if you've read the book, you'd already know that a Babel Fish is able to decode any language in the universe. In the game, then, you'll know what to look for when confronted with an alien language (Adams and Meretzky 1984). In The Enterprise Incidents, the player must solve a word puzzle whose solution, the word *firefly*, is not mentioned elsewhere in the game. (Desilets 2002) In Goldilocks is a FOX, knowledge of fairy tales is required to solve puzzles involving magic beans, bears, and porridge. (Guest 2002) Sherlock contains intricate riddle poems whose solutions are allusions to famous historical figures buried in Westminster Abbey. The player is also required decode a riddle poem and realize that references to "the conquest" and "the fire" refer to the Battle of Hastings and the Great Fire of London, respectively. Finally, the player is expected to know the dates for these two dates in order to subtract one from the other in order to solve a puzzle. (Bates 1987) A number of modern text-based games (Curses, OMNIQUEST, All Quiet on the Library Front, Inhumane, and the later Zork games, to name a few) play off of established text adventure tropes, clichés, and catchphrases (common passwords across games include "XYZZY" and "Plugh" from Cave Adventure (Crowther and Woods 1976), and magic spells learned in the Enchanter series carry over from game to game, although they have to be 'learned' in-game in order to be used).

Self-Maintenance. Hunger, thirst, fatigue are the most common survival elements in text adventures. Players might have to keep space open in their inventory for food and drink, and will be prompted from time to time that they are getting hungry or thirsty, or that they might need to rest. Similar obstacles that pop up are: hypothermia (when swimming in Zork III (Infocom 1982)), the classic lamp from Zork (Infocom 1980) (which reappears and is innovated on in the sequels, where it can go out if you neglect to shake it or turn it back on), and torches from Infidel (which you are required to regularly dip in oil and light) (Berlyn 1983). One complication of self-maintenance is whether the action is one time or continuous (in Infidel, for example, you need to gather food and drink, but once they're gathered, you have an unlimited amount).

Combat. Combat can come in a variety of forms. At its most basic level, a player will be confronted with an enemy and can thwart it by typing `kill enemy`. To complicate things further, the player might not be equipped to kill the enemy with their bare hands, and must first acquire a weapon before `kill enemy` will return "`enemy killed`". One level higher, the player might have to `attack enemy` and `dodge enemy` or `aim at X` (where X = a weak spot you learn about elsewhere in the game) before killing the enemy. Higher levels include stochastic combat (where attacks may or may not land), optional combat (where the only solution to the fight is to avoid it) and puzzle combat. In Reverberations, for example, the player encounters an enemy in the cosmetics section of a department store. To win the fight, the player must spray the enemy with some nearby perfume. (Glasser 1996)

Time. In Wishbringer, the player has a limited amount of time at the start of the game to deliver a note. The player must use this time to collect items and information that will be inaccessible once they've delivered the note. (Moriarty 1985) In Sherlock, the player is given 48 hours of in-game time to solve the mystery. Certain locations and events are only accessible at certain times. (Bates 1987)

Mechanical Puzzle. Some examples can be found in Infidel and Inhumane, where the player has to move objects around a room, leave objects in rooms, and prop open doors with wooden beams in order to avoid being caught in traps. (Berlyn 1983) (Plotkin 1985)

Persistence. In some games, Anchorhead for example, you must repeat talk to commands in order to get more information out of an NPC. (Gentry 1998)

Stochasticity. Some examples of stochasticity include randomly generated maze configurations, randomly decided combat action outcomes, and randomly selected code-words for puzzles. Text-based game players deal with stochasticity with the UNDO action or by saving often and especially right before taking any kind of risky action.

Cruelty Scale. The Cruelty Scale was designed by text-based game author Andrew Plotkin as a broad method of determining the difficulty of text-based games. The main element considered by the scale is whether or not the game can be made impossible to win, and how obvious (or not) this is made to the player. The scale has five ranks: Merciful games are impossible to die or get stuck in, Polite games warn you before you do something that can kill or trap you or otherwise render the game unwinnable. Tough games can kill the player or be rendered unwinnable, but they'll warn the player before this happens. Nasty games can be rendered unwinnable without warning, but there will be an indication that the game is now unwinnable after the fact. Cruel games can be rendered unwinnable, and there's no warning beforehand and no indication afterwards.

Length. Text-based games vary wildly in length, from the solvable-in-twenty-moves inform demo Acorncourt to the 1000+ moves required to complete Anchorhead, text-based games have many elements that impact their length. These include: Number of possible commands, number of rooms, length of descriptive text, (Reverberations, for example, is solvable with a relatively low number of commands (roughly 50), but features long descriptive passages for almost every room and command) side quests and multiple endings, and game difficulty. However, text-based game review sites and discussion boards often divide games up into short demo type games, medium uncomplicated games, and long difficult games.

B   Curated List of Text-Based Games

See Table 2.

Table 2. Information we collected during our analysis of text-based games.

Game	# Rooms	Max score	Maze	Trivia	Self-maintenance	Combat	Time	Mechanical Puzzle	Persistence	Stochasticity	Forgiveness
The Acorn Court	1	30	No	No	No	No	No	Yes	No	No	Merciful
Adventure	30+	350	Yes	Yes	No	Yes	Yes	Yes	Yes	No	Tough
Adventureland	30+	100	Yes	Yes	No	Yes	Yes	Yes	Yes	Yes	Tough
All Quiet on the Library Front	2+	30	No	Yes	No	No	No	No	No	No	Merciful
Anchorhead	30+	100	No	Yes	No	Yes	Yes	No	Yes	No	Cruel
The Awakening	30+	50	No	Yes	No	Yes	Yes	No	Yes	No	Polite
Balances	10+	51	No	Yes	No	No	No	Yes	Yes	No	Polite
Ballyhoo	30+	300	Yes	Yes	Yes	No	No	Yes	No	Yes	Tough
Curses	30+	550	No	Yes	No	No	Yes	No	Yes	Yes	Polite
Cutthroat	30+	250	Yes	No	Yes	Yes	Yes	Yes	Yes	Yes	Polite
Deephome	10+	300	Yes	No	No	Yes	Yes	Yes	Yes	No	Polite
Detective	10+	360	No	No	No	Yes	No	No	No	No	Cruel
Dragon Adventure	2+	25	No	No	No	Yes	No	No	No	No	Merciful
Enchanter	30+	400	Yes	No	Yes	Yes	Yes	Yes	Yes	Yes	Cruel
The Enterprise Incidents	10	10	No	Yes	No	No	Yes	No	Yes	No	Merciful
Goldilocks is a FOX!	30+	100	Yes	Yes	No	No	No	Yes	No	No	Polite
The Hitchhiker's Guide to the Galaxy	30+	100	Yes	Yes	Yes	No	No	Yes	Yes	Yes	Cruel
Hollywood Hijinx	10+	150	Yes	Yes	No	Yes	No	Yes	No	No	Nasty
Infidel	10+	400	Yes	Yes	Yes	No	No	Yes	No	No	Cruel
Inhumane	10+	400	Yes	Yes	No	Yes	No	Yes	No	No	Polite
The Jewel of Knowledge	30+	90	Yes	No	No	Yes	No	Yes	Yes	Yes	Tough
Leather Goddesses of Phobos	30+	316	Yes	Yes	No	Yes	No	Yes	Yes	Yes	Cruel
Mother Loose	10+	50	No	Yes	No	No	No	No	No	No	Merciful
Lost Pig	2+	7	No	No	No	No	No	Yes	No	No	Merciful
The Ludicorp Mystery	30+	150	Yes	No	No	No	Yes	Yes	No	No	Polite
The Lurking Horror	10+	100	Yes	No	Yes	Yes	Yes	Yes	Yes	No	Polite
The Meteor, the Stone and a Long Glass of Sherbet	30+	30	No	Yes	No	Yes	Yes	No	No	Yes	Cruel
Monsters of Murdac	30+	250	Yes	No	No	Yes	Yes	No	No	Yes	Nasty

(continued)

Table 2. (continued)

Game	# Rooms	Max score	Maze	Trivia	Self-maintenance	Combat	Time	Mechanical Puzzle	Persistence	Stochasticity	Forgiveness
Night at the Computer Center	10+	10	Yes	Yes	No	No	No	No	No	No	Merciful
OMNIquest	2+	50	No	Yes	No	Yes	No	No	No	No	Polite
Pentari	2+	70	No	No	No	Yes	Yes	No	No	Yes	Polite
Planetfall	10+	80	No	No	Yes	Yes	Yes	Yes	Yes	Yes	Polite
Plundered Hearts	10+	25	No	Yes	No	Yes	Yes	Yes	No	No	Polite
Return to Karn	30+	170	No	Yes	No	No	Yes	Yes	Yes	Yes	Nasty
Reverberations	10+	50	No	Yes	No	Yes	Yes	Yes	No	No	Polite
Seastalker	30+	100	No	No	No	Yes	Yes	Yes	Yes	No	Nasty
Sherlock: The Riddle of the Crown Jewels	30+	100	No	Yes	No	Yes	Yes	Yes	Yes	Yes	Nasty
Sorcerer	10+	400	Yes	Yes	Yes	Yes	Yes	Yes	Yes	Yes	Nasty
Spellbreaker	30+	600	Yes	Yes	No	Yes	Yes	Yes	Yes	Yes	Cruel
Spiritwrak	30+	250	Yes	Yes	Yes	Yes	Yes	Yes	Yes	Yes	Polite
The Temple	10+	35	No	Yes	No	Yes	Yes	No	Yes	No	Polite
Theatre	30+	50	No	Yes	No	Yes	Yes	Yes	Yes	No	Polite
Trinity	30+	100	Yes	Yes	No	No	Yes	Yes	No	Yes	Tough
Tryst of Fate	30+	350	Yes	Yes	No	Yes	Yes	Yes	Yes	Yes	Polite
Wishbringer	30+	100	Yes	No	No	Yes	Yes	Yes	Yes	Yes	Tough
Zenon	10+	20	No	No	No	No	Yes	No	No	No	Polite
Zork I	30+	350	Yes	Yes	Yes	Yes	Yes	Yes	Yes	Yes	Cruel
Zork II	30+	400	Yes	Yes	Yes	Yes	Yes	Yes	No	No	Cruel
Zork III	30+	7	Yes	Yes	Yes	Yes	Yes	Yes	Yes	Yes	Cruel
Zork: The Undiscovered Underground	10+	100	Yes	Yes	No	No	Yes	Yes	Yes	Yes	Tough

B.1   Game Notes

Below are observations for some of the games we analyzed.

The Acorn Court Written as an Inform demo. Very short game with only one room. Contains one multi-part spatial puzzle.

Adventure First IF. Difficult, stochastically generated mazes, introduces made up words. We used the recompiled with Inform 6 (release 9) version which starts with an initial score of 36 points.

Anchorhead Heavily text based. Requires a combination of world knowledge and knowledge gleaned from in-game texts. When speaking with townspeople, you have to occasionally be persistent. Awareness of Lovecraftian cliches is helpful.

Balances Another Inform demo, features made up words and spells that the player must remember. Rare words used in the context of magic and fantasy are also used.

Deephome Medium length game with an in game library the player can consult in order to figure out the solutions to puzzles.

Dragon Adventure Short game written to introduce children to text based games.

Detective Poorly written game. Navigation isn't very logical (you can walk east into a room whose only exit is to the north). Gameplay is very simple - you only need to use navigation commands to reach the end of the game.

Enchanter Long game with a complex spell-casting system that requires player to memorize and record spells.

Goldilocks is a FOX! Requires trivia knowledge (you need to know about Jack and the Beanstalk in order to know what to do when someone offers you magic beans). Casual language with lots of pop cultural references.

Hitchhiker's Guide to the Galaxy Incredibly difficult to play. Several stochastic obstacles (A maze without a set solution, An object from a subset of objects is randomly made into a crucial object). Features many irrational objects and events, including objects showing up in your inventory without warning. Leans on world knowledge a bit as well, as when the navigation controls change to Port, Starboard, Aft, and Bow/Fore. Some puzzles are solvable if you are familiar with the books. Language is also sarcastic and, at times, deliberately misleads the player.

Infidel Many spatial puzzles. Draws on world knowledge (player must decode hieroglyphics and pictograms). Instruction manual contains the navigation instructions for finding the pyramid. Contains some potential one-way paths (you need to tie a rope to an object in one room in order to re-enter it).

Inhumane Parody of infidel but with a more straightforward, simpler map. Has a meta game where you try to nearly solve puzzles and then kill yourself. Some familiarity with Infidel makes playing it easier. Contains some clue-hunting that doubles as room unlocking, you can also find directions through a maze in the game. Contains a gag ending triggered by entering s instead of south or vice versa as your final command. There are mazes, but there are also some unconnected rooms that have identical names (T-Intersections appear in different areas).

All Quiet on the Library Front Relatively simple treasure hunt with minimal side-quests and Easter eggs. Contains some text-based game in-jokes that do not impact the gameplay, but might be distracting.

Lost pig Game text is written in "cave-person speak". Otherwise a simple pig hunt with some magic spell based puzzles.

The Lurking Horror Medium length game that requires you to understand which rooms are above which other rooms in order to guess the solution to a puzzle.

Spiritwrak Features a massive map with a working subway system. Uses an Enchanter-style spell system.

Trinity Long game with surreal imagery. Map made of several sub-worlds linked through a central hub.

Sherlock: The Riddle of the Crown Jewels Very dependent on world knowledge. Time based. Some word puzzles. Player can easily get stuck in an unwinnable state without knowing it, and is expected to have a familiarity with Victorian England and British history and culture and general.

Wishbringer Designed for beginner players. Features a hint system and an object that grants the player "wishes" that help them bypass puzzles.

Zork I Classic text-based game treasure hunt with dungeon theme. In addition to the treasure hunt component, player has to contend with a thief, combat with a troll, and navigate a maze. Knowledge about *The Odyssey* can help the player defeat a Cyclops.

Zork II Sequel to Zork I. Contains a maze modelled after a baseball diamond that confused some European players when first released.

Zork III Sequel to Zork II. High score can be achieved without winning the game. Game rewards the player for finding innovative solutions to problems rather than for solving puzzles, navigating to rooms, or retrieving objects.

C   Inform 7

Inform refers to a domain-specific programming language and additional tooling for interactive fiction (*i.e.*, text-based games). It is regarded as the most natural language-like programming language. It was originally created in 1993 by Graham Nelson and he later released Inform 7 (briefly known as Natural Inform). We decide to use Inform7 so we could leverage Inform's impressive parser that benefited from more than two decades of tweaks/fixes. Inform 7 source compiles to Inform 6 source, a weakly-typed multiple-inheritance traditional programming language, before compiling to Z or glulx code. See http://inform7.com/ for more information on Inform 7. Also, here is a supplemental resource for some of the technical details: http://www.ifwiki.org/index.php/Inform_7_for_Programmers.

References

Adams, D., Meretzky, S.: The Hitchhiker's guide to the galaxy (1984). http://ifdb.tads. org/viewgame?id=ouv80gvsl32xlion

Atkinson, T., Baier, H., Copplestone, T., Devlin, S., Swan, J.: The text-based adventure AI competition. arXiv preprint arXiv:1808.01262 (2018)

Baroni, M., et al.: CommAI: evaluating the first steps towards a useful general AI. arXiv preprint arXiv:1701.08954 (2017)

Bates, B.: Sherlock: the riddle of the crown jewels (1987). http://ifdb.tads.org/ viewgame?id=j8lmspy4iz73mx26

Beattie, C., et al.: DeepMind Lab. arXiv preprint arXiv:1612.03801 (2016)

Bellemare, M.G., Naddaf, Y., Veness, J., Bowling, M.: The arcade learning environment: an evaluation platform for general agents. J. Artif. Intell. Res. (JAIR) **47**, 253–279 (2013)

Bengio, Y., Louradour, J., Collobert, R., Weston, J.: Curriculum learning. In: Proceedings of the 26th Annual International Conference on Machine Learning, pp. 41–48. ACM (2009)

Berlyn, M.: Infidel (1983). http://ifdb.tads.org/viewgame?id=anu79a4n1jedg5mm

Brockman, G., et al.: OpenAI Gym. arXiv preprint arXiv:1606.01540 (2016)

Chaplot, D.S., Sathyendra, K.M., Pasumarthi, R.K., Rajagopal, D., Salakhutdinov, R.: Gated-attention architectures for task-oriented language grounding. arXiv preprint arXiv:1706.07230 (2017)

Chomsky, N.: Three models for the description of language. IEEE Trans. Inf. Theory **2**(3), 113–124 (1956). https://doi.org/10.1109/tit.1956.1056813

Crowther, W., Woods, D.: Aventure (1976). http://ifdb.tads.org/viewgame? id=fft6pu91j85y4acv

Desilets, B.: The enterprise incidents (2002). http://ifdb.tads.org/viewgame? id=ld1f3t5epeagilfz

Fikes, R.E., Nilsson, N.J.: STRIPS: a new approach to the application of theorem proving to problem solving. Artif. Intell. **2**(3–4), 189–208 (1971)

Fulda, N., Ricks, D., Murdoch, B., Wingate, D.: What can you do with a rock? Affordance extraction via word embeddings. arXiv preprint arXiv:1703.03429 (2017)

Galley, S., Lawrence, J.: Seastalker (1984). http://ifdb.tads.org/viewgame? id=56wb8hflec2isvzm

Genesereth, M., Love, N., Pell, B.: General game playing: overview of the aaai competition. AI Mag. **26**(2), 62 (2005)

Gentry, M.: Anchorhead (1998). http://ifdb.tads.org/viewgame?id=op0uw1gn1tjqmjt7

Glasser, R.: Reverberations (1996). http://ifdb.tads.org/viewgame?id=dop7nbjl90r5 zmf9

Guest, J.J.: Goldilocks is a FOX! (2002). http://ifdb.tads.org/viewgame?id=59ztsy9p0 1avd6wp

Haroush, M., Zahavy, T., Mankowitz, D.J., Mannor, S.: Learning how not to act in text-based games. In: International Conference on Learning Representations - Workshop (2018)

He, J., et al.: Deep reinforcement learning with a natural language action space. arXiv preprint arXiv:1511.04636 (2015)

Henderson, M., Thomson, B., Williams, J.D.: The second dialog state tracking challenge. In: Proceedings of the 15th Annual Meeting of the Special Interest Group on Discourse and Dialogue (SIGDIAL), pp. 263–272 (2014)

Hermann, K.M., et al.: Grounded language learning in a simulated 3D world. arXiv preprint arXiv:1706.06551 (2017)

Infocom. Zork I (1980). http://ifdb.tads.org/viewgame?id=0dbnusxunq7fw5ro

Infocom. Zork III (1982). http://ifdb.tads.org/viewgame?id=vrsot1zgy1wfcdru

Kaelbling, L.P., Littman, M.L., Cassandra, A.R.: Planning and acting in partially observable stochastic domains. Artif. Intell. **101**(1–2), 99–134 (1998)

Kempka, M., Wydmuch, M., Runc, G., Toczek, J., Jaśkowski, W.: ViZDoom: a doom-based AI research platform for visual reinforcement learning. In: 2016 IEEE Conference on Computational Intelligence and Games (CIG), pp. 1–8. IEEE (2016)

Kostka, B., Kwiecieli, J., Kowalski, J., Rychlikowski, P.: Text-based adventures of the Golovin AI agent. In: 2017 IEEE Conference on Computational Intelligence and Games (CIG), pp. 181–188. IEEE (2017)

Machado, M.C., Bellemare, M.G., Talvitie, E., Veness, J., Hausknecht, M., Bowling, M.: Revisiting the arcade learning environment: evaluation protocols and open problems for general agents. arXiv preprint arXiv:1709.06009 (2017)

Martens, C.: Ceptre: a language for modeling generative interactive systems. In: Eleventh Artificial Intelligence and Interactive Digital Entertainment Conference (2015)

McFarlane, R.: A survey of exploration strategies in reinforcement learning (2003). https://www.cs.mcgill.ca/~cs526/roger.pdf

Mnih, V., et al.: Human-level control through deep reinforcement learning. Nature **518**(7540), 529–533 (2015)

Moriarty, B.: Wishbringer (1985). http://ifdb.tads.org/viewgame?id=z02joykzh66wfhcl

Narasimhan, K., Kulkarni, T., Barzilay, R.: Language understanding for text-based games using deep reinforcement learning. arXiv preprint arXiv:1506.08941 (2015)

Parisotto, E., Salakhutdinov, R.: Neural map: structured memory for deep reinforcement learning. arXiv preprint arXiv:1702.08360 (2017)

Pearson, K.: The problem of the random walk. Nature **72**(1867), 342 (1905)

Plotkin, A.: Inhumane (1985). http://ifdb.tads.org/viewgame?id=wvs2vmbigm9unlpd

Puterman, M.L.: Markov Decision Processes: Discrete Stochastic Dynamic Programming, 1st edn. Wiley, New York (1994). ISBN 0471619779

Russell, S.J., Norvig, P.: Artificial Intelligence: A Modern Approach. Pearson Education Limited, Kuala Lumpur (2016)

Ryan, J., Seither, E., Mateas, M., Wardrip-Fruin, N.: Expressionist: an authoring tool for in-game text generation. In: Nack, F., Gordon, A.S. (eds.) ICIDS 2016. LNCS, vol. 10045, pp. 221–233. Springer, Cham (2016). https://doi.org/10.1007/978-3-319-48279-8_20

Sukhbaatar, S., Szlam, A., Synnaeve, G., Chintala, S., Fergus, R.: MazeBase: a sandbox for learning from games. arXiv preprint arXiv:1511.07401 (2015)

Sutton, R.S., Barto, A.G.: Reinforcement Learning: An Introduction. MIT Press, Cambridge (2018)

Wright, W.: SimCity. Erbe (1996)

General Game Playing

Statistical GGP Game Decomposition

Aline Hufschmitt[(✉)], Jean-Noël Vittaut, and Nicolas Jouandeau

LIASD, University of Paris 8, Saint-Denis, France
{alinehuf,jnv,n}@ai.univ-paris8.fr

Abstract. This paper presents a statistical approach for the decomposition of games in the *General Game Playing* framework. General game players can drastically decrease game search cost if they hold a decomposed version of the game. Previous works on decomposition rely on syntactical structures, which can be missing from the game description, or on the disjunctive normal form of the rules, which is very costly to compute. We offer an approach to decompose single or multi-player games which can handle the different classes of compound games described in *Game Description Language* (parallel games, serial games, multiple games). Our method is based on a statistical analysis of relations between actions and fluents. We tested our program on 597 games. Given a timeout of 1 h and few playouts (1k), our method successfully provides an expert-like decomposition for 521 of them. With a 1 min timeout and 5k playouts, it provides a decomposition for 434 of them.

Keywords: General Game Playing · Decomposition ·
Game description langage · Causality · Compound moves · Serial games

1 Introduction

Solving smaller sub-problems individually and synthesizing the resulting solutions can greatly reduce the cost of search for a general game player. Previous works on compound games show this and propose some approaches to solve pre-decomposed single games [3,5] or multi-player games [12]. Sum of games has been widely studied to solve games with specific complete decomposition [1]. However, identifying such sub-problems is an essential prerequisite. In this paper we focus on the decomposition of games described in *Game Description Language*(GDL).

We identify different classes of compound games [7] which raise specific issues for decomposition: *games using a stepper* like *Asteroids*[1], *synchronous* or *asynchronous* [3] *parallel games* respectively like *Chinook*[2] or *Double Tictactoe*

---

[1] In *Asteroids* the player must drive a small spaceship (in up to 50 steps) to an asteroid and stop on it. If the ship stops before reaching the destination, the game ends with the score 0.

[2] Chinook is composed of two games of Checkers disputed on the white cells and the black cells of the same board.

© Springer Nature Switzerland AG 2019
T. Cazenave et al. (Eds.): CGW 2018, CCIS 1017, pp. 79–97, 2019.
https://doi.org/10.1007/978-3-030-24337-1_4

Dengji[3], *synchronous parallel games with compound moves* like *Snake-Parallel*[4], *serial games* like *Factoring-Turtle-Brain*[5], *multiple games* like *Multiple-Sukoshi*[6] and *impartial games starting with several piles of objects* like *Nim*[7].

Some characteristics of these games represent specific difficulties for decomposition. *Serial games* are games with sequential subgames: when a subgame terminates, another subgame starts. The second game is strongly linked to the first one as the start of the second game depends on the first game state. *Compound moves* are single actions that are responsible of effects related to different subgames; the separation of these effects is critical to separate the subgames.

The *Game Description Language* used to described general games is a logic language similar to Prolog which uses the closed world assumption and uses negation as failure. The logical rules used to infer fluents that will be true in the next state, given a partial description of the current state and a joint move of the players, do not explicitly describe action effects. In the premises of these rules, with head predicate *next*, some fluents describe some aspect of the current state necessary for the rule head to be entailed but not a complete state. Therefore the exploration of each game state from initial state is necessary to know exactly in which state these rules can be entailed and what is the effect of actions. For example, frame axioms indicate fluents that keep a true value from one state to another given some specific actions: actions not present in these frame rules are those susceptible to have a negative effect. However, among those, some may be illegal when the rule applies. To identify these illegal actions, it is necessary to acquire high level knowledge on the game to know that premises necessary for action legality are incompatible with a premise of the preceding rules. However, like it has been demonstrated with STRIPS-descriptions in planning domain [2], a complete inference of all mutually exclusive fluents is intractable for complex games.

In this paper we propose a statistical approach based on simulation to identify the action effects and to decompose the different classes of compound games mentioned above. We first present the previous works on decomposition (Sect. 2) then define what is a correct decomposition of a game (Sect. 3). We present the different aspects of our method to handle the different types of compound games (Sect. 4). We present experimental results on 597 games (Sect. 5). Finally, we conclude and present future work (Sect. 6).

---

[3] At each turn a player chooses a *Tictactoe* grid from two to place one of his marks. The goal is to win in both grids.

[4] The goal of *Snake* is to move, for 50 steps, a snake that grows steadily without biting its tail.

[5] Factoring Turtle Brain is a series of *LightsOn* games where the player has to turn on 4 lights: each lamp goes out gradually while he lights up the others.

[6] *Sukoshi* is about creating a path by aligning ordered integers. In the *multiple* version only one grid counts for the score, the others are useless.

[7] In *Nim* each player takes in turn any number of matches in one of 4 stacks. Whoever no longer has a match to pick loses.

```
(role r)
(light a) (light b) (light c) (light d)
(<= (legal r (push ?x)) (not (true (on ?x))) (light ?x))
(<= (next (on ?x)) (does r (push ?x)))
(<= (next (on ?x)) (true (on ?x)))
(<= terminal (true (on a)))
(<= (goal r 0) (not (true (on b))) (not (true (on c))))
(<= (goal r 40) (true (on b)) (not (true (on c))))
(<= (goal r 60) (not (true (on b))) (true (on c)))
(<= (goal r 100) (true (on b)) (true (on c)))
```

Fig. 1. Minimalist game represented in GDL. The player can light 4 lamps. Turn on a ends the game. It only gets the maximum score if b and c are lit at the end.

2   Previous Works

We assume familiarity of the reader with General Game Playing [4] as well as with the Game Description Language (GDL) [8]. A GDL game description takes the form of a set of assertions and logical rules. A set of keywords allows to describe the game. Figure 1 give an example of GDL description. Keywords are represented in bold. The syntax (<= a x ... y) means that a is true if the conjunction of premises $x \wedge ... \wedge y$ is true; the variables are indicated by a question mark. The *legal* predicate specify the legality of an action; *next* rules indicate conditions under which a fluent is true in the next state; *terminal* signals if the current state is a game end; *goal* completes the score reached by the player if the current state is terminal. Rules are expressed in terms of actions (*does*) and fluents (*true*) describing the game state.

To quickly evaluate the rules and carry out simulations of the game (*play-outs*), Vittaut et al. [11] propose a fast instantiation using Prolog with tabling that builds a rule graph similar to a propnet [9]. This rule graph is transformed into a logic circuit [10] which can be quickly evaluated using binary operators. This circuit uses the head of *legal*, *next*, *goal* or *terminal* rules as outputs, and fluents (*true*) and actions (*does*) as inputs.

Günther et al. [6] propose a decomposition approach for single player games by building a *dependency graph* between uninstantiated fluents and actions nodes: the connected components of the graph represent the different subgames. Edges are potential preconditions, positive and negative effects between fluents and actions while action-independent fluents are isolated in a separate subgame to prevent them from joining all subgames. Their program is tested on the game *Incredible*.

Zhao et al. [13] present an extension of this approach to multi-player games using partially instantiated fluents and actions in the *dependency graph*. Serial games and compound move games are treated separately [12] and their detection heavily rely on game description syntactic structures: rewriting some GDL rules can prevent decomposition. For serial games, they use a separate specific detection: a predicate like *game1over* in *Tictactoe Serial* which is false in the *legal* rules of the first subgame and true in the *legal* rules of the second one is used to split the game. Results are presented on the games *Nim*, *Double CrissCross2* and several variants of *Tictactoe* (*Double*, *Serial*, *Parallel*).

In [7], we propose an approach which is more general but also off-line like the aforementioned ones. It relies on weak heuristics to identify the effects of actions: effects not explicitly described are ignored and can induce over-decomposition. To solve the problem of the compound moves, we identify meta-actions sets which represent a single effect of a compound move: a compound move with N effects is part of N meta-action sets and actions with a single effect are meta-action singletons. These meta-actions are sets of actions which have an identical effect on a fluent of a particular subgame in the same conditions i.e. with the same preconditions in the rules describing the next state and with at least one fluent in common to precondition their legality. However this detection requires the costly calculation of completely developed disjunctive normal form (DNFD) of the game rules. The detection of serial games is limited to two subgames. To separate them, this approach looks for expressions capable of partitioning the legality of actions into two groups. The approach also detect *useless* subgames i.e. with no influence on score, game termination and, in the case of serial subgames, not allowing another *usefull* subgame to start. We consider actions of these games as *noop* actions that can receive the same evaluation during the game exploration. This decomposition is tested on 40 games: 7 games from trivial (*Tictactoe*) to complex (*Hex*) and 33 compound games representative of the different classes presented.

To limit the computation time, another version uses partially developed disjunctive normal form (DNF): auxiliary predicates are preserved as atoms and are not completely developed. The decomposition using the DNF is quicker: for some games, time decreases from one hour with DNFD to one second with DNF (Fig. 8). However this version is less robust: depending on the rules formulation, meta-action detection can fail as well as decomposition. Note that both versions fail to correctly decompose *Chomp* and *Blocker Parallel* is not decomposed after a one-hour timeout.

In this paper, we propose a more robust detection of action effects based on statistical information collected during playouts. We use a circuit encoding the game rules to perform fast simulations and collect information on the correlation between fluent value changes and actions played. This circuit is also used to infer preconditions relations using propagation and back-propagation of different signals. We propose a concept of *crosspoint* which allows to detect junctions between independent parts of a game played sequentially and allows to decompose serial games with any number of subgames. Our approach does not require the use of DNF. We tested our approach on significantly more games than previous works (597 against 1,4 and 40).

3   Game, Subgame and Correct Decomposition

A game is described by a finite state machine the structure of which is a directed acyclic graph. Let F be the set of the fluents. A state is a set $s \subset F$. A transition is a couple $(s, s') \subset F^2$.

A decomposition is a tuple $F_1, \ldots F_n$ where $\bigcup_{i=1}^{n} F_i = F$ and $\forall i, j, i \neq j :$ $F_i \cap F_j = \emptyset$.

In a subgame i a state is a set $s_i \subset F_i$ and a transition is a couple $(s_i, s_i') \subset F_i^2$ such that there exists a transition $(s, s') \subset F^2$ in the global game where $s_i = s \cap F_i$ and $s_i' = s' \cap F_i$.

Definition 1 (free choice of a transition). *Given a state $s = s_1 \cup s_2$ of a global game where s_1 is a state of the first subgame and s_2 a state of the second subgame, we can freely choose a transition (s_1, s_1') in the first subgame and (s_2, s_2') in the second one, if, in the global game, there exists a transition $(s_1 \cup s_2, s_1' \cup s_2')$ or a sequence of transitions $(s_1 \cup s_2, s_1' \cup s_2)$ followed by $(s_1' \cup s_2, s_1' \cup s_2')$.*

Definition 2 (compatible decomposition). *The decomposition of a game in two subgames is compatible with the global game if in any subgame it is possible to choose freely a transition from a state to a distinct one.*

The extension of Definitions 1 and 2 to more than two subgames is straightforward.

Definition 3 (correct decomposition). *A decomposition is* correct *if it is compatible with the global game and there exists independent victory conditions (evaluation function) in the subgames such that winning every subgames implies winning the global game.*

In the example given in Fig. 1, each lamp can be placed in a separate subgame: a transition can be freely chosen to switch on one of the lamps and independent evaluation functions are identifiable because each lamp involved in the calculation of the score provides a portion of the points.

In games with a binary score (win or loose), like *Nonogram*, evaluation functions can nevertheless be identified as the condition of victory is composed of distinct subgoals.

Given the aforementioned definitions, we however consider that a game like *Nine Board Tictactoe* is not decomposable. In this game consisting of 9 *Tictactoe* board arranged in 3 rows by 3 columns, each mark of a player in the cell of index i of a given board determines the following board i where the opponent will have to replicate, the aim being to align 3 marks in one of the board. Transitions depend on previous moves and can not be chosen freely if each board is a subgame. A game like *Blocker* is also non-decomposable. In this game, played on a 4×4 board, *Crosser* must put his mark in the cells to build a bridge across the board while *Blocker* tries to block the road with its own marks. Even though it is possible to freely choose the transitions in the 16 subgames consisting of only one cell of the global game, there do not exist independent victory conditions allowing to evaluate the score in one cell subgames. A single marked cell can be part of a winning state as well as a loosing one.

4   Method

To identify the different subgames we create a dependency graph; nodes are meta-action sets (see Definition 8 and Sect. 4.4) and completely instantiated fluents; edges represent effect or precondition relationships between them. We compute edge weights to allow the identification of lightly connected parts of the graph (Sect. 4.7). Construction of this graph is detailed in Sect. 4.6. The identified connected components represent the subgames.

For the analysis of relations between fluents and actions, we use the following definitions:

Definition 4 (premises). *Let F be the set of all the instantiated fluents and $f \in F$ a given positive or negative fluent. Let R be the set of all roles r. Let A be the set of all instantiated players actions $a = (does\ r\ o)$. Let h be the head of a variable free GDL rule. $g \in F \cup A$ is a **premise** of h if:*

- *g is in the body of this rule, or*
- *g is in the body of a variable free GDL rule of head i and i is a premise of h.*

*g is an **non-conflicting precondition** of h if no conflict exists between g and another premise of h i.e. if h is satisfiable when g is true.*

*g is an **exclusive precondition** of h if $g \Rightarrow h$ i.e. if h is true when g is true whatever the value of the other premises of h.*

As action effects are not explicitly described in GDL rules, we define an *effect* as a phenomenon the cause of which is not known a priori and observed during a transition:

Definition 5 *A **positive effect** f^+ (resp. **negative effect** f^-) is the value change of a fluent f from false (resp. true) in a state, to true (resp. false) in the next state. Let f^* represents a given effect (positive or negative) on $f \in F$.*

Some effects always happen simultaneously with other effects; we distinguish between two sorts of co-occurring effects:

Definition 6 (Globally co-occurring effects (GCE)). *$GCE(f^*)$, the set of globally co-occurring effects of f^* consists of effects that always occur together with f^* regardless the actions that caused this effect on f. Let $|GCE(f^*)|$ be the number of times this co-occurrence is observed during the playouts.*

Definition 7 (Action co-occurring effects (ACE)). *$ACE(a, f^*)$, the set of co-occurring effects of f^* for an action a, consists of effects occurring always together with f^* when the action a is played. Let $|ACE(a, f^*))|$ be the number of times this co-occurrence is observed during the playouts.*

A meta-action is a set M of actions responsible for the same effects f^* in the same circumstances. These circumstances correspond to fluents necessary for the actions legality, i.e. the premises of the *legal* rule for each $a \in M$, but also to the premises used in conjunction with theses actions $a \in M$ in the body of the rules of head (next f). These rules indicate whether the conditions are met for the action to have an effect. Identifying the actions occurring with the same set of preconditions in the different clauses of a rule of head (next f) requires the calculation of the disjunctive normal form of this rule. However, by a comparison of all sets of actions occurring with each precondition taken separately, it is also possible to identify these actions.

Actions with no effect on f^* but used in conjunction with the same fluent g in the premises of (next f), correspond to a set $A' = A - (M \cup I)$ with A given at the Definition 4, M a meta-action set with an implicit effect f^* and I a set of illegal actions under the same conditions. These illegal actions may belong to another subgame than f: in this case, the meta-action sets that have an effect on the fluents of the other subgame are included in I. The comparison of actions sets with a same effect, with actions sets with a same precondition in a next rule, and with actions sets with a same precondition in their legal rule, allows to identify meta-action sets even if the effects are not explicitly described in the GDL rules.

We therefore propose the following definition of meta-action sets which does not require rule DNF:

Definition 8 *A meta-action set $M(r, \mathcal{E}, \mathcal{N}, \mathcal{L})$ is a set of actions of role r such that all the following conditions are verified:*

- $\mathcal{E} \neq \emptyset$ *and for each $f^* \in \mathcal{E}$, f^* is an effect of each $a \in M(r, \mathcal{E}, \mathcal{N}, \mathcal{L})$.*
- *for each fluent $g \in \mathcal{N}$ and for each action $a \in M(r, \mathcal{E}, \mathcal{N}, \mathcal{L})$, g is used in conjunction with a in the premises of (next f) with $f^* \in \mathcal{E}$, and a is not an exclusive precondition of (next f).*
- *for each fluent $h \in \mathcal{L}$ and for each action (does r o) $\in M(r, \mathcal{E}, \mathcal{N}, \mathcal{L})$, h is a non-conflicting precondition of (legal r o). $\mathcal{L} = \emptyset$ if (legal r o) is always true for each action (does r o) $\in M(r, \mathcal{E}, \mathcal{N}, \mathcal{L})$.*
- *there does not exist $A' \subsetneq M(r, \mathcal{E}, \mathcal{N}, \mathcal{L})$ such that for each $a' \in A'$, a fluent g' is used in conjunction with a' in the premises of (next f'), a' is not an exclusive precondition of (next f') and a' has no effect on f'.*

To decompose serial games, we are looking for a state or group of states that are necessarily visited during the game. No action sequence allows to reach the rest of the game without going through one of these states. They can be characterized by the presence of a *crosspoint*: one specific fluent or a conjunction of fluents. For example, in *Blocker Serial* composed of two games of *Blocker* played one after the other, the fluent game1overlock signals the end of the first subgame and conditions the legality of the actions of the second subgame. In *Asteroids Serial*, composed of two games of *Asteroids*, the first subgame ends when the spaceship stops, which is represented by the conjunction of fluents (north-speed1 0) ∧ (east-speed1 0) indicating a zero speed on the 2 cardinal axes. These *crosspoint* can be identified from a *causal graph* representing the causal relationships between actions and fluents. Each fluent inside a *crosspoint* is a *crosspoint component*:

Definition 9 *Let G be a causal graph i.e. a directed graph representing the causal relationships between the actions and the fluents (positive or negative) of a game. Given $C(G)$ the transitive closure of G, a fluent node x is a* **crosspoint component** *if in $C(G)$:*

- *there exists at least one edge to the node x, and*
- *there exists at least one edge from x to an action node, and*
- *x is not in the initial state of the game.*

Let a **crosspoint** *X be a set of at least one* **crosspoint component**.

4.1   Simulation Based Detection of Action Effects

Our approach uses a statistical estimation of the number of action effects during random playouts. Thus our playouts are gathering information to build the decomposition. At each step of the game, each player indicates its move; the set of all of these actions constitutes a joint move. In an alternate move game, only one player has the choice between multiple legal moves while the other player actions have no effect (often named *noop*). For each transition in a playout, the joint move is associated with state changes. After a given number of simulations, for each action a that occurs in $|J(a)|$ distinct joint moves, we estimate the probability $\mathbb{P}(a, f^+)$ that a positive effect on fluent f follows action a:

$$\mathbb{P}(a, f^+) = (\sum_{0 < i < |J(a)|} \frac{E(J(a)_i, f^+)}{O(J(a)_i)})/|J(a)|$$

with $J(a)$ the set of joint moves containing action a, $O(J(a)_i)$ the number of occurrences of a given joint move of this set during playouts and $E(J(a)_i, f^+)$ the number of times a positive effect on f has been implied by this joint move. The probability that a negative effect f^- follows the action a, is defined similarly.

$\mathbb{P}$ indicates the probability to observe a change when an action is played. However the change of some fluents like *step* or *control* does not depend on actions and some actions like *noop* have no effect on any fluents. The formulation of the rules does not always make it possible to detect them. For example, the presence of a *noop* action in the premises of the rules describing the next state of a *control* or *step* fluent can prevent detection.

4.2   Filtering Action Effects

A positive value of $\mathbb{P}(a, f^*)$ does not indicate if there is an effect of a on f or a simple correlation. A second step in identifying action effects is therefore needed to check each potential effect suggested by a positive value of $\mathbb{P}(a, f^*)$ to filter effects and eliminate correlations.

We first detect alternate moves: our purpose is to detect *noop* actions with no effects and action-independent *control* fluent. A n-player game is a sequential game when for each state $n - 1$ players have only one legal action which is therefore considered as *noop*. The fluent that most frequently change when a *noop* action is played is the corresponding *control* fluent, which allows to detect it. If the only actions present in the premise of some fluents are *noop* actions then these fluents are considered action-independent.

For each action a, we then check each potential positive or negative effect given by the probability $\mathbb{P}(a, f^*)$ to confirm or deny the link between a and f^*. By observing the rules of the game, it is possible to decide if a rule describes an explicit action effect or if it implies a possible effect. If no such rule is present in the GDL description of the game, we can assume that the action cannot have a positive effect on the fluent: we then set the probability to zero.

For example, an *explicit positive effect* of an action (does r o) on the fluent f is described by a GDL rule like (<= (next f) (does r o) (not (true f))) where f changes from false in the premises to true when action (does r o) is chosen. A rule like (<= (next f) (not (does r x)) (not (true f))) can suggest that action (does r o) has an *implicit positive effect*. Rules like (<= (next f) (does r o)) or (<= (next f) (not (does r x))) which both do not indicate if the fluent f is supposed to be true or not in the current state, can also implies a positive effect of (does r o). Similarly, the absence of certain rule patterns can be checked to eliminate negative effects.

By examining the co-occurring effects, we can also filter effects which cannot be the result of some actions. We reconsider the different co-occurring effects of each eliminated effect to detect erroneously assigned ones until no more is filtered. An action a cannot be the cause of an effect f^* if $\mathbb{P}(a, g^*) = 0$ with $g^* \in GCE(f^*)$. On the contrary, the effect f^* of a is confirmed if there exists a g^* with $\mathbb{P}(a, g^*) > 0$ and either $g^* \in GCE(f^*)$ with $|GCE(f^*)| > \Psi$ or $g^* \in ACE(a, f^*)$ with $|ACE(a, f^*)| > \Theta$, where Ψ and Θ are thresholds necessary to only consider true co-occurring effects (sufficiently tested during playouts) and eliminate false positives. If an effect f^* can be confirmed for some actions a but not for the other actions, we consider that other actions are not the cause of this effect.

For multi-player games we also compare the probabilities of the effect attributed to the different actions of a joint move. If an action a of a joint move has a probability Φ times greater than another action b to be followed by the effect f^* then the cause of the effect is a and we update $\mathbb{P}(b, f^*)$ to a zero value. If the same change occurs for any transition from initial state and never in any other transition, it is considered independent of actions. When no more effect can be eliminated, if no action is the cause of a fluent change, this fluent is flagged as action-independent.

4.3   Action Independent Fluents

We use the circuit, to identify the preconditions of action independent fluents. We back-propagate 4 possible states (*undefined, true, false* or *both*) from each (next f) output where f is an action-independent fluent to flag its different premises. Then, for each activated positive or negative fluent input, we check if the fluent can change f from *false* to *true* (in this case, it is really a precondition, not a conflicting one) or if it can force f to remain true: then the inverse value of the fluent has a negative effect on f.

4.4 Compound Moves and Meta-action Sets

To identify the meta-action sets according to Definition 8, we use the previous detection of action effects and consider that $\mathbb{P}(a, f*) > 0$ denotes an effect of a on f. We detect action preconditions in *legal* and *next* rules using the logic circuit built from the rules.

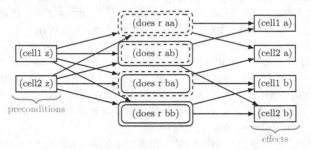

(a) Identification of action groups with a same precondition and responsible of a same effect.

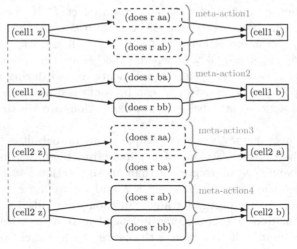

(b) Separation of meta-actions

Fig. 2. Graphic representation of meta-actions identification. Fluents with *cell1* predicate belong to the first subgame, those with predicate *cell2* belong to the second one. The identification of meta-actions allows to remove the links between fluents of both subgames.

To find each fluent h that is a premise of a legal rule of head (legal r o), we set the output (legal r o) to *true* and back-propagate the signal into the circuit with four possible states in the same way as in Sect. 4.3. We then check that each of these fluents actually allows the action to be legal using a three state propagation in the circuit i.e. it is a *non-conflicting precondition* (Definition 4).

To find each fluent g used in conjunction with an action a in the premises of (next f), we set the input (does r o) to *true* and propagate the signal through the circuit without taking care of the logic gates to label each gate depending on this action including some *next* outputs. Then we back-propagate the signal from the (next f) output using different flags to specifically label the gates representing a conjunction between the action and another input (according De Morgan law it can be an *or* gate inside a negation) and mark the fluent inputs used in these conjunctions.

Then we compare the different action sets with a same effect, with a same precondition in a next rule or with a same precondition in their legal rule and recursively split each set until we find the meta-action sets (Fig. 2).

4.5   Serial Games and *crosspoints* Identification

To identify the *crosspoints* from the *crosspoint components* set as defined in Definition 9, we build a *causal graph* G where nodes are actions, positive or negative fluents. As the logical relations between nodes are represented by directed edges, we add an edge $y \to z$ in G if:

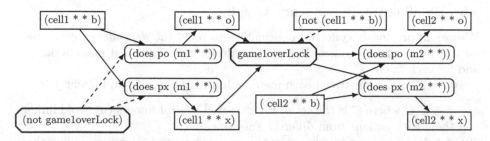

Fig. 3. Extremely simplified *causal graph* for the game *Tictactoe Serial*. m1, m2, po and px stand respectively for *mark1, mark2, playero* and *playerx*. A set of terms with variable arguments is represented using wildcards *. Some links are omitted to clarify the graph. *Game1overLock* is identified as a *crosspoint*.

(1) y is an action and z is the result of an effect of y;
(2) y is a fluent (maybe action-independent) premise of (legal r p) with $z =$ (does r p);
(3) y is a fluent, z is an action and $y \wedge z$ are premises of (next f) where f^* is an effect of z;
(4) y is a premise of (next z) where z is an action-independent fluent.

A single *crosspoint component* x is a *crosspoint* if there do not exist two edges $x \to y$ and $y \to x$ in $C(G)$. For example, Fig. 3 shows a very simplified version of the *causal graph* obtained for the game *Tictactoe Serial*. The fluent *game1overLock* marks a clear boundary between two distinct parts of the game and is a *crosspoint*.

Given X_c the set of identified *crosspoint components*, a set $X_i \subset X_c$ is a *crosspoint* candidate in $C(G)$, if there exists a set of nodes Q such that, forall $x \in X_i$ and forall $q \in Q$, there exists an edge $x \to q$. For each X_i which is a *crosspoint* candidate, we add a node o_i in G. Then we use the circuit to identify the logical relations between each node o_i and other nodes. In G, we add an edge $y \to o_i$ for each edge $y \to x$ with $x \in X_i$ and we add an edge $o_i \to y$ if:

(1) an action $y = $ (does r p) is legal when all $x \in X_i$ are true and there exist $x \in X_i$ where x is a premise of (legal r p);
(2) (next f) is possibly true when all $x \in X_i$ are true and there exist $x \wedge y$ premises of (next f) where f^* is an effect of the action y;
(3) y is an action independent fluent and y^* is entailed when all $x \in X_i$ are true.

X_i is a crosspoint if there do not exist two edges $o_i \to y$ and $y \to o_i$ in $C(G)$.

A *crosspoint* is discarded if it has another *crosspoint* or a fluent of the initial state has a unique precondition or if it includes another *crosspoint*.

4.6   Building the Dependency Graph

We use all previously collected information to build the *dependency graph* necessary to identify subgames. We add a node for each identified meta-action M and for each fluent f[8].

We add an edge between each meta-action $M(r, \mathcal{E}, \mathcal{N}, \mathcal{L})$ and fluent f if:

(1) $f \in \mathcal{L} \backslash C$ where C is the set of the detected *control* fluents (to avoid linking them with actions from different subgames);
(2) $f \in \mathcal{N} \backslash C'$ where C' is the set of the detected *control* fluents or, failing that, the set of all action-independent fluents;
(3) $f^* \in \mathcal{E}$.

Edges (1) and (2) receive a weight of 1. The weight W of edges (3) is the mean of the action effect probabilities: $W = \sum_{0<i<N} \frac{\mathbb{P}(a_i, f^*)}{N}$ with $a_i \in M(r, \mathcal{E}, \mathcal{N}, \mathcal{L})$.

We also add an edge for each precondition of an action-independent fluent. To separate the serial subgames, we remove the links between each fluent present in a *crosspoint* and the fluents or actions that are preconditioned by this *crosspoint*.

Some actions may not have been tested and some fluents change may have never been observed during playouts. These actions and fluents are considered to belong to all subgames until additional playouts provide more information.

---

[8] Positive fluent (true f) and negative fluent (not (true f)) are represented by the same node in the dependency graph.

4.7   Subgoals to Fix Under- or Over-Decomposition

In some games, there does not exist a relationship between some internal structures outside of the game goals. It is the case for cells in *Tictactoe*, columns in *Connect Four*[9] or colored regions in *Rainbow*[10]. Conversely, in a game like *Lights On Parallel*[11], we would like to separate the four groups of lamps as lighting one of them is sufficient to achieve victory. But, as each action of lighting a lamp has a negative collateral effect on all other lamps (they gradually go dark), a logical link exists in our dependency graph that connects subgames.

To solve these two problems, we collect *subgoals* using the circuit. The logic gates of the goal sub-circuit are sorted such that if the output of a gate is used as an input of another one it is examined first.

Each logic gate p of the sub-circuit is activated independently of the others with a value $o \in \{true, false\}$ and, using a three state logic to broadcast the signal, the state of the goal outputs is examined. If an output with the maximum score for one of the players is activated, then the value o of the gate p represent a *victory condition*. Otherwise, if a non-zero score can nevertheless be obtained (the score 0 is false, a score greater than 0 is true or the value $\neg o$ makes the maximum score impossible to achieve), then the value o of the gate p represents a *subgoal*. Each gate, the output value of which depends on a previously detected *subgoal*, is removed from the *subgoal* search: this allows to collect only the minimal conditions necessary to obtain a non zero score. We proceed similarly for *victory conditions*.

If several action-dependent subgames are detected, i.e. if the *dependency graph* presents several subgraphs containing action nodes, we check if the game is not over-decomposed. We verify that each detected subgoal or victory condition does not depends on fluents which are in different subgames. If this happens, the subgames are combined into one. It also allows us to verify that a subgame, if its fluents are involved in the calculation of the score, makes it possible to obtain at least a portion of the points.

If only one action dependent subgame is detected, it can group several subgames each allowing to obtain a maximum score but joined by collateral effects of the actions. To check if such subgames exist, we remove all effects links the weight of which is less than the threshold Ω from our *dependency graph* and then the *victory conditions* are used as before to join the parts of the game forming subgames guaranteeing the victory.

---

[9] In *Connect Four* players drop colored tokens from the top into a seven-column, six-row vertically suspended grid. The goal is to align 4 tokens.

[10] *Rainbow* is a puzzle that consists in coloring a map such that no adjacent regions have the same color.

[11] Four game of *LightsOn* are played in parallel by a single player who chooses in which subgame he wishes to act on each turn. The player gets 100 points if he wins any of the 4 subgames.

5   Experiments

There is no expert data specifying what the expected decomposition is for each of the game descriptions in the repositories. According to the definitions in Sect. 3, we have therefore established for 597 games found in the *Base, Stanford* and *Dresden* repositories of http://games.ggp.org/[12], the expected number of action-dependent and action-independent subgames with the number of useless ones[13]. But as it is possible to separate a game into N parts in different ways, in each of our experiments, we manually checked each decomposition with more than 1 subgame to ensure that it agrees with Definitions 1, 2 and 3[14].

The experiments are performed on one core of an Intel Core i7 2.7 GHz with 8Go of 1.6 GHz DDR3. The value for the ratio and thresholds are empirically set to the following values: $\Psi = 3$, $\Theta = 5$, $\Phi = 1.5$ and $\Omega = 0.1$. These parameters are not sensitive to slight variations. For example, the value of Ψ leads to ignoring co-occurring effects during the first Ψ observations: the value of Ψ must be high enough to rule out coincidences but paranoid value will just require a larger number of playouts to achieve the same result.

For each game, we measure the time necessary to build the circuit, execute 5k playouts and process the decomposition. Figure 4 shows that 70% of the games can be decomposed in less than 1 min, a time compatible with GGP competitions setup. Most of the time is used for the creation of the circuit. For example, once the circuit is created, 35 s are sufficient to collect initial information, execute 5k playouts and decompose *Blocker Parallel* that was not decomposed by previous works. 40 games are not decomposed before the 1 h timeout, among them 32 are decomposable (Fig. 6).

5 kp	<1s	<10s	<30s	<1min	<3min	<10min	<30min	<1h
total	72	307	391	434	491	527	540	557

Fig. 4. Number of games for which the stage of the decomposition is reached in the given time (for 5k *playouts*).

The decomposition time and the grounding time are not correlated i.e. a game description producing a lot of grounded rules do not take necessarily more time to decompose. However, if the game tree is more complex, all actions and their effects may not be tested during the 5k playouts used to collect information therefore the decomposition is less reliable.

The decomposition process can be reiterated when more simulations have been performed. In Fig. 5, we evaluate the number of correct decompositions

---

[12] We excluded GDL-II descriptions using the *sees* predicate.

[13] These data are available upon request to the main author.

[14] Note that an expert-like decomposition may not equal a correct decomposition. For example, a human expert would like to decompose *Nine Board Tictactoe*. However such a decomposed game would be difficult to solve.

obtained after each group of 1k playouts. We find that 1k playouts are enough to properly decompose 87% of the games. The only under-decomposed game after 10k playouts (Fig. 6) is *Simultaneous Win 2* for which no subgoal (evaluation function) could be identified for the subgames.

	1kp	2kp	3kp	4-6kp	7kp	8kp	9-10kp
under-decomp.	9	5	4	2	2	2	1
decomposed	521	525	527	529	530	532	533
over-decomp.	26	26	25	25	24	22	22

Fig. 5. Number of games correctly decomposed after 1k to 10k playouts.

result after 10kp	compound	single
under-decomposed	1	-
decomposed	349	182
over-decomposed	20	5
timeout (1h)	32	8
total	402	195

Fig. 6. Number of games correctly decomposed or not after 10k playouts among compound games or single games.

The result of the decomposition after 10k playouts is presented for compound and single games separately (Fig. 6). The over-decomposition is, in a majority of cases, due to the lack of information; more playouts would allow a proper decomposition. For example, in *Snake* or *Tron*, a part of the game board is not explored during playouts and constitutes a separate subgame.

Other cases of over-decomposition are observed for games that consist in surviving for a number of steps (*Queens, Max-Knights*[15]): a wrong move ends the game and the score depends on the current step. In this case, the role of the main game is poorly detected: only the stepper is considered usefull. In some games with simultaneous moves like *Point Grab*[16] or *Smallest*[17], each player is placed in a separate subgame: the identified subgoals do not link the actions of both players. Some games are more problematic: in *Roshambo*[18] or *Beat Mania*[19], an

---

[15] The goal of *Queens* or *Max-Knights* is to place a given number of queens or knights on a chessboard so that no chessman threatens another.

[16] *Point Grab* is played in 30 steps. At each step, 2 players have the choice between different useless actions or grab a point a or a point b. If both player choose the same point, nobody wins.

[17] *Smallest* is a game played in a maximum of 25 steps. At each step, four player choose simultaneously a number. The player with the strictly smallest one wins 5 points.

[18] *Roshambo* consists of 10 rounds of rock/paper/scissors/well.

[19] *Beat Mania* is a 2 player game. The first player loose blocks from 3 different positions and the other must catch them. Each missed or caught block earns points to the corresponding player.

effect of actions is to increment a *counter* composed of several fluents. The effect on each separate fluent is not significant and action effects are not correctly detected. A concept of *meta-effect* on a set of fluents would be necessary to handle such games.

All the decomposable games for which the decomposition could not be obtained in less than an hour, consist of a stepper associated with an action-dependent subgame. The time required to create the circuit leaves almost no time for decomposition. For these games, an *ad-hoc* detection of a *stepper* could allow to obtain a decomposition more rapidly.

Interesting decompositions are obtained for games of *Nonogram* (5 × 5 and 10 × 10) the status of several cells can be decided independently of the others and fluents and actions related to these cells are isolated in independent subgames (Fig. 7). The remaining part of the board is decomposed in several subgames if the mark to be placed in cells does not depend on the rest of the game. These decompositions would allow to solve the game much more rapidly.

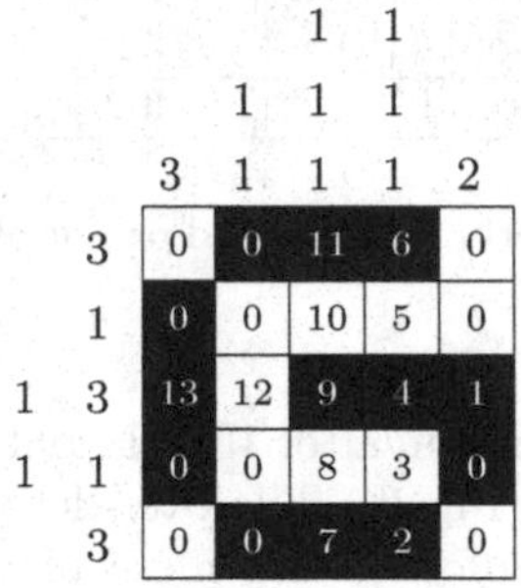

Fig. 7. Graphic representation of the decomposition obtained for the game *Nonogram* 5 × 5. The number in each cell represents the subgame to which it belongs.

We have compared the result of our decomposition with previous works [6,7,13]: we obtain a correct decomposition for all the game tested in the afore-mentioned papers[20]. No measure of decomposition time is indicated by Günther et al. [6] and Zhao et al. [13]. Figure 8 parallels the results obtained in [7] with the results obtained for the statistical approach presented in this article; it should be noted that the DNF approach, although faster than the DNFD, is much less reliable and heuristics used to detect causal links with both approaches are very weak. Unlike this previous approach, we obtain a correct decomposition for *Chomp* and *Blocker Parallel* within less than 1 h.

---

[20] We do not test *Double Crisscross 2* which is not available in repositories.

Jeu	DNFD	DNF	stats
Blocker Parallel	>1hr	>1hr	≈48min
Asteroids	<1sec	<1sec	<2sec
EightPuzzle	<2sec	<2sec	≈3sec
Checkers	>1hr	<12min	≈28min
Breakthrough	<16min	<16min	≈14sec
Sheep and wolf	>1hr	<5sec	≈6sec
Tictactoe	≈1sec	<1sec	<1sec
Nineboardtictactoe	>1hr	<2sec	<17sec
Tictactoex9	>1hr	<5sec	≈11sec
Chomp	<1sec	<1sec	<2sec
Multiplehamilton	<1sec	<1sec	<2sec
Multipletictactoe	<10sec	<1sec	≈1sec
Blockerserial	<20min	<10min	≈3sec
Dualrainbow	≈1min	<8sec	≈6sec
Asteroidsparallel	<1sec	<1sec	≈2sec
Dualhamilton	<1sec	<1sec	<2sec
Dualhunter	<2sec	<2sec	<3sec
Asteroidsserial	<1sec	<1sec	<4sec
LightsOnParallel	<8min	<1sec	<1sec
LightsOnSimul4	<8min	<1sec	≈3sec
LightsOnSimultaneous	<8min	<1sec	≈3sec
Nim3	<2sec	<2sec	<2sec
Chinook	<14sec	<14sec	≈21sec
Double tictactoe dengji	>1hr	<1sec	<1sec
SnakeParallel	>1hr	<2sec	<7sec
TicTacToeParallel	>1hr	≈2sec	<2sec
Doubletictactoe	>1hr	<1sec	<1sec
TicTacHeaven	>1hr	<2sec	≈17sec
TicTacToeSerial	>1hr	<1sec	<1sec
ConnectFourSimultaneous	>1hr	<1sec	<2sec
DualConnect4	>1hr	<1sec	<2sec
Jointconnectfour	>1hr	<1sec	<2sec

Fig. 8. Comparison of results from [7] (DNFD, DNF) with those obtained with our statistical approach (stats) for 32 games among the 40 they tested. Results of the 3 approaches are identical for the 8 remaining games.

6   Conclusion and Future Work

We presented a simulation based game decomposition approach we tested on a large set of games. This approach provides a solution to the problem of identifying the effects of actions. The analysis of information collected during playouts allows to identify the explicit and implicit actions effects. It also allows to detect alternate moves or *steppers* when the rule formulation tries to hide them. We proposed an approach for the decomposition of serial games based on the identification of some *crosspoints* inside the game. We show also that it is possible to identify meta-actions without resorting to the disjunctive normal form of rules, which is very costly to compute. We can then decompose a game like *Breakthrough* which was not decomposed in less than 1 h in previous works.

We tested our approach on 597 games from http://games.ggp.org/. Our results demonstrate that it is possible to transform the GDL rules into a logic circuit, execute 5k playouts and process the decomposition in less than 1 min for 70% of the games. We also show that 1k playouts are sufficient to obtain a correct decomposition for 87% of the games.

Decompositions presented here are computed from the initial state of the game. As a decomposition can be enhanced when more information is available (more playouts are done), it is possible to detect fluents the value of which changes once and for all in each new state, to use this information to remove some links in the *dependency graph* and to discover new decompositions while playing.

We have seen that some games present specific difficulties: games where action effects on each fluent is not significant like in *Roshambo* or *Beat Mania* or in which the goal is to survive N steps like in *Queens* or *Max-Knights*. Our decomposition approach cannot handle games with fluents or actions shared between several subgames like *Tic-Block* or *Factoring-Mutually-Assured-Destruction*. We will investigate in the future how to handle these games without significantly increasing computational cost for all games.

Approaches that synthesize subgame solutions to better solve a global game are restricted to certain types of games that can easily be decomposed in an ad-hoc way (puzzles or 2-player synchronous parallel games). As our approach allows to obtain a decomposition sufficiently robust on a wide range of games in a time compatible with the *General Game Playing* competition setup, our first objective is to develop a player using the result of this decomposition to increase its strength.

References

1. Berlekamp, E., Conway, J., Guy, R.: Winning Ways for your Mathematical Plays, vol. 2. Academic, Cambridge (1982)
2. Blum, A., Furst, M.L.: Fast planning through planning graph analysis. Artif. Intell. **90**(1–2), 281–300 (1997)
3. Cerexhe, T., Rajaratnam, D., Saffidine, A., Thielscher, M.: A systematic solution to the (de-)composition problem in general game playing. In: Proceedings of ECAI, pp. 1–6 (2014). http://cse.unsw.edu.au/~mit/Papers/ECAI14.pdf
4. Genesereth, M.R., Love, N., Pell, B.: General game playing: overview of the AAAI competition. AI Mag. **26**(2), 62–72 (2005). http://aaaipress.org/ojs/index.php/aimagazine/article/download/1813/1711
5. Günther, M.: Decomposition of single player games. Master's thesis, TU-Dresden (2007). http://www.inf.tu-dresden.de/content/institutes/ki/cl/study/assignments/download/beleg_guenther_subgame_detection.pdf
6. Günther, M., Schiffel, S., Thielscher, M.: Factoring general games. In: Proceedings of the IJCAI-09 Workshop on General Game Playing (GIGA 2009), pp. 27–33 (2009). http://www.general-game-playing.de/downloads/GIGA09_factoring_general_games.pdf

7. Hufschmitt, A., Vittaut, J.-N., Méhat, J.: A general approach of game description decomposition for general game playing. In: Cazenave, T., Winands, M.H.M., Edelkamp, S., Schiffel, S., Thielscher, M., Togelius, J. (eds.) CGW/GIGA -2016. CCIS, vol. 705, pp. 165–177. Springer, Cham (2017). https://doi.org/10.1007/978-3-319-57969-6_12. http://giga16.ru.is/giga16-paper3.pdf

8. Love, N., Hinrichs, T., Haley, D., Schkufza, E., Genesereth, M.: General game playing: game description language specification. Technical report LG-2006-01, Stanford University (2008)

9. Schkufza, E., Love, N., Genesereth, M.: Propositional automata and cell automata: representational frameworks for discrete dynamic systems. In: Wobcke, W., Zhang, M. (eds.) AI 2008. LNCS (LNAI), vol. 5360, pp. 56–66. Springer, Heidelberg (2008). https://doi.org/10.1007/978-3-540-89378-3_6

10. Vittaut, J.N.: LeJoueur: un programme de General Game Playing pour les jeux à information incomplète et/ou imparfaite. Ph.D. thesis, Université Paris 8 (2017)

11. Vittaut, J.N., Méhat, J.: Fast instantiation of GGP game descriptions using prolog with tabling. In: Proceedings of ECAI, pp. 1121–1122 (2014)

12. Zhao, D.: Decomposition of multi-player games. Master's thesis, TU-Dresden (2009). http://www.inf.tu-dresden.de/content/institutes/ki/cl/study/assignments/download/dengji_zhao_master_thesis.pdf

13. Zhao, D., Schiffel, S., Thielscher, M.: Decomposition of multi-player games. In: Nicholson, A., Li, X. (eds.) AI 2009. LNCS (LNAI), vol. 5866, pp. 475–484. Springer, Heidelberg (2009). https://doi.org/10.1007/978-3-642-10439-8_48. http://cgi.cse.unsw.edu.au/~mit/Papers/AI09b.pdf

Iterative Tree Search in General Game Playing with Incomplete Information

Armin Chitizadeh$^{(\boxtimes)}$ and Michael Thielscher

UNSW Sydney, Kensington, NSW 2052, Australia
{a.chitizadeh,mit}@unsw.edu.au

Abstract. General Game Playing (GGP) is concerned with the development of programs capable of effectively playing a game by just receiving its rules and without human intervention. The standard game representation language GDL has recently been extended so as to include games with incomplete information. The so-called Lifted HyperPlay technique, which is based on model sampling, provides a state-of-the-art solution to general game playing with incomplete information. However, this method is known not to model opponents properly, with the effect that it generates only pure strategies and is short-sighted when valuing information. In this paper, we overcome these limitations by adapting the classic idea of fictitious play to introduce an Iterative Tree Search algorithm for incomplete-information GGP. We demonstrate both theoretically and experimentally that our algorithm provides an improvement over existing solutions on several classes of games that have been discussed in the literature.

Keywords: General game playing with incomplete information ·
Learning · Valuing information · Fictitious play

1 Introduction

Designing a player for games with incomplete information[1] has been studied in different areas. Vector minimax is a well-known and relatively general technique, which has been shown to solve the so-called strategy-fusion problem [6]. A limitation of the vector minimax technique is to rely on a specific game structure: It is limited to games in which all the moves can be seen except the first ones by the random player, e.g. where cards are being shuffled [4]. Another relatively general technique for playing incomplete-information games is Information Set Monte Carlo Tree Search (ISMCTS) [2]. This technique generalizes the well-known Monte Carlo tree search to incomplete-information games. Thanks to the

---

[1] In game theory the term *imperfect information* is used to refer to the class of games in which players lack full information about the state of the game. On the other hand, in AI it is more common to use the expression *incomplete information* for problems in which agents lack full information. It has become customary in GGP to follow the standard AI terminology.

© Springer Nature Switzerland AG 2019
T. Cazenave et al. (Eds.): CGW 2018, CCIS 1017, pp. 98–115, 2019.
https://doi.org/10.1007/978-3-030-24337-1_5

use of Monte Carlo simulations, this technique performs well for large games. One of its limitation is given by the assumption that all states in an information set are equally likely. Due to this limitation, ISMCTS fails to properly model opponents or to play games with non-uniform probability distributions over possible states such as the famous Monty Hall problem [9]. Counterfactual Regret Minimization (CFR) [23] was introduced to solve the imperfect-information game of poker. This technique performs well thanks to poker specific optimisations [12]. However, its general implementation failed to perform equally well in other games with incomplete information. One of the reasons is the high computational complexity of $\mathcal{O}(I^2N)$, where I is the number of information sets and N the total number of states in the game [13]. All of the previously mentioned techniques perform well in some games, but it is believed that their success relies heavily on game-specific expertise of their developers and tailored algorithms.

More recently, AlphaZero [20] was able to learn the game of chess from scratch and through self-play to a point where it was able to beat Stockfish [16], the hitherto best chess engine. AlphaZero uses a relatively general approach compared to its predecessor AlphaGo [20]. However, AlphaZero is only applicable to complete-information two-player board games [20].

General Game Playing is concerned with the development of an AI capable of playing any arbitrary finite game effectively by just receiving the rules of the game without any human intervention. GGP programs receive the game rules in the form of the general Game Description Language (GDL), which has a Prolog-like syntax [14]. The first version of GDL was designed to only model deterministic games with full observability. Later, the extension GDL-II was developed for general game playing with incomplete information [21]. This extended general specification language allows to describe any finite game with incomplete information and randomness, for example, Poker or Backgammon, to a general game-playing system; however, designing such a system has remained a challenge.

The first successful players for GGP-II approached the problem by grounding all unknown variables and generating a set of sampled complete-information game states. They then searched each state sample and averaged the reward for moves over each of them in order to find the optimal move [3,17]. However, searching on a set of sampled complete-information states for a game with incomplete information has its limitations, as pointed out in a recent paper on a technique called lifted HyperPlay [18]. Specifically, when searching separate complete-information samples, no extra value be put on moves that provide additional information about the current game state. This was a limitation of all previous approaches that combined search with complete-information sampling and was the main motivation for the development of the two state-of-the-art techniques in general game playing with incomplete information: HyperPlayer with Incomplete Information (HP-II) [18] and the so-called Norns algorithm [8].

HP-II uses nested players to simulate games. Through this technique, it can value knowledge-gathering moves, and it can also value moves that prevent the opponents from gaining helpful knowledge. However, this comes at the price of two main limitations of HP-II itself: high resource consumption [19] and, more importantly, short-sightedness when it comes to valuing information, as we will demonstrate in this paper. The aforementioned Norns algorithm, which uses Action-Observation Trees (AOT) to simulate a game and to determine the value of information, also suffers from high resource consumption and, more importantly, is restricted to single-player games [8].

In this paper, we introduce *Iterative Tree Search* (ITS) to overcome the limitations of HP-II and Norns. Our main motivation was to find a technique that, in principle, can correctly solve GDL-II games in general provided their search space is suitably small, rather than finding a technique that is applicable to large games. Our ITS combines the classic idea of *fictitious play* [1] with incomplete information tree search. Fictitious play learns the behavior of a rational opponent by self-playing a game several times. Incomplete information tree search is able to model an information set at every step of the game.

The main contributions of our paper are as follows: We formally introduce Iterative Tree Search as a new approach to general game playing with incomplete information. We theoretically analyse both the ITS and the HP-II algorithm and show the limitations of HP-II compared with ITS on different classes of games. We also report on experimental results with an implementation of the ITS algorithm to demonstrate its advantages over the existing techniques.

2   Background

In this section, we will briefly describe General Game Playing with Incomplete Information (GGP-II) and Fictitious Play (FP). For further details we refer the reader to [18] and [1].

2.1   General Game Playing with Incomplete Information

Players in General Game Playing (GGP) are given the rules of a game in the declarative Game Description Language (GDL) [14]. States in GDL are defined as sets of true facts. The initial state and terminal states are distinguished, and rewards are given to players at terminal states. In GDL-II, Nature is modeled as a special-purpose "random" player. This player chooses its moves at random with uniform probability, and it has the same reward values at all terminal states. Logical rules are used to describe the legal actions and their effects on a game state. In GDL-II, players' moves are hidden from each other, but players may receive "observation tokens" after each joint move [21]. The only way of learning something about the moves by other players is through these perceptions. Rules of the game explicitly describe under which conditions a player makes an observation. When the game ends, players will be notified and are given a reward value. In GGP, by convention the minimum reward value is 0 and the maximum reward value is 100. The goal of players is to achieve the maximal reward.

Formalisation. In this paper, we will not be concerned with a set of GDL rules themselves but rather consider the induced game tree, including players' perceptions [21]. GDL and GDL-II allow us to describe games with simultaneous moves. For simplicity of explanation, we will use the standard transformation by which joint-move incomplete-information games in GGP-II can be converted into sequential incomplete-information games.

Definition 1. *Let* $G = \langle S, R, M, \Sigma, s_0, Z, u, do \rangle$ *be a game with incomplete information, where:*

- *S is a set of states;*
- *R is a set of players, and $R(s)$ is a function which given state s provides the player whose turn it is;*
- *M is a set of moves, and $M(s)$ is the list of legal moves at state s by the player[2];*
- *Σ is a set of perceptions, and $\Sigma(s)$ is the list of perceptions for $R(s)$ from initial state to s;*
- *$s_0 \in S$ is the initial state of the game;*
- *$Z \subset S$ is the set of terminal states, for which we have $M(z) = \emptyset$ for any $z \in Z$;*
- *$u : Z \to \Re^{|R|}$ is the terminal utility function;*
- *$do : S \times M \to S$ is the successor function.*

To illustrate this, we look at an extended cutting wire game (ECW), adapted from a cooperative game presented in [18] and which we use later in Sect. 4.1. Figure 1 shows the left part of the game tree. The roles are $R = \{random, cutter, teller\}$. At first, the random player arms a bomb, and only the teller sees which of two wires is used for this purpose. For the next two moves, then, the teller can either decide to tell which wire was used, or wait. Telling first costs 20 points and telling later costs 10 points for both players. Through telling, the cutter is informed about which wire he should cut to disarm the bomb. At the end, the cutter has to decide which wire to cut. Cutting the correct one gives both players 100 points (minus the aforementioned costs). Otherwise, they get 0. We use the sequence of moves as subscript to denote a state in the game tree, for example s_{rtwr}. Examples for the set of legal moves and list of percepts for a state are: $M(s_{rw}) = \{wait2, tell2\}$ and $\Sigma(s_{rtt}) = [(), red, red]$ respectively. As the cutter reaches its decision state s_{rtt}, he has received three perceptions along the path. The first perception is empty because the first action by random does not result in any perception for the cutter. The second and third both are "*red*" because, in this particular state, the teller has chosen *tell1* and *tell2*. The final utility in this case $u(s_{rttr}) = 70$. The $do(S, M)$ function returns the next state, e.g. $d(s_r, wait) = s_{rw}$.

---

[2] Each move is unique. Having similar names for moves at different states does not mean the moves are the same.

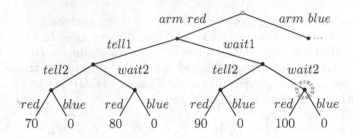

Fig. 1. Part of the game tree for the extended "cutting wire" game, with the red wire being armed. The green circle means the node is in an information set together with one other node in the other half of the game tree (because the cutter has not received any observation token). (Color figure online)

2.2 Fictitious Play

In game theory, fictitious play has been suggested as a learning technique [1]. It was originally designed for one step joint-move games, that is, normal form games. It is known to find a Nash equilibrium (NE) in the time-average sense for two-player zero-sum games, for games solvable with iterated strict dominance, and for so-called identical interest games as well as potential games [15]. Recently, the technique has been extended to some sequential-form games, for example, full-width extensive-from fictitious play (XFP) [10] and neural fictitious self-play (NFSP) [11]. The XFP technique learns a strategy which is realization-equivalent to the normal form fictitious play, meaning it considers a strategy as a whole. For this reason, this technique suffers from the curse of dimensionality. The NFSP technique uses sampling and neural networks to learn an NE strategy for the game. It was able to play limited Texas Hold'em successfully, but this game has no information-gathering moves.

The standard fictitious play updates a mixed policy after each iteration by averaging the previously played moves [1]. The updating algorithm can be mathematically described as follow:

$$\pi_r^{t+1} = \frac{\pi_r^t}{t} + \frac{\pi(b(\pi_{-r}^t))}{t+1} \tag{1}$$

Here, r is the player and t is the iteration index. π_r^t is the mixed policy for player r at iteration t and π_{-r} is the mixed policy for all players except r. Mixed policy π_r defines the probabilities for player r to choose a move at each state where it is this player's turn.

Given the mixed policy π_{-r} of other players, player r finds the best response as follows:

$$b(\pi_{-r})^t = \underset{m \in M}{\mathrm{argmax}}\ util(m, \pi_{-r}^t) \tag{2}$$

Here, $b(\pi_{-r})$ is the best-response function which returns the best move m_r for player r given the mixed policy for the other players; and $util(m_r, \pi_{-r})$ is the reward function for player r if he plays move m given the strategy π_{-r} for the opponents. In this paper, we refer to π as a function which takes a move and returns a policy with the probability of the given move being 1 and all others being 0.

3 Iterative Tree Search

In this section, we will introduce a novel algorithm called the Iterative Tree Search (ITS) for GGP-II. ITS is an offline search, meaning it finds the best move before the game begins, and then during the game, it plays based on the pre-calculated mixed move policy. We first need to generate the incomplete-information tree and initialize its probabilities and utilities of the states; then we need to update the states' values and move probabilities iteratively, all within the given time limit before the start of the game.

3.1 Initialising the Tree

The first step in initialising the incomplete-information game tree is to represent indistinguishability of states. We use information sets for this purpose, which can be determined from the observation tokens a player has received [21].

Definition 2. *Let G be a GDL-II game as in Definition 1, then:*

- *$I(s) : S \rightarrow S^*$ is the information set function which takes a state s and returns a set of states. The given state and all the states in the returned set are indistinguishable by the player for whom s is a decision node.*

Since we are converting games into sequential form, the player for which states are indistinguishable is always the player whose turn it is. The following equation describes formally how an information set is generated:

$$I(s) = \{x \in S \ : \ \Sigma(s) = \Sigma(x) \wedge \xi_r(s) = \xi_r(x) \wedge r = R(s)\} \tag{3}$$

Here, $\xi_r : S \rightarrow M^*$ is the *history* function which provides the sequence of moves of player r from the start to the provided state. In our ECW example, the only non-singular information set is $I(s_{rww}) = \{s_{rww}, s_{bww}\}$. We refer to this information set as I_{ww}.

Our ITS technique assigns probabilities to moves and states in each information set. The probability of a state can be recursively calculated from the probabilities of the moves. Through iteratively updating both probabilities, we can obtain a mixed strategy for every information set in a game tree that can be used to play optimally during the game.

When initializing the tree, we provide uniform probability to the moves in a state. A mixed policy is beneficial in a sense that it can prevent the opponent from predicting our moves. In the ECW example, the first iteration will be the initial move probability of $\mu(tell1) = \frac{1}{2}$.

3.2 Iterative Probability Update

After populating the probabilities of the moves, we calculate the probability of every state in an information set to be the true state of the game.

Definition 3. *Let G be a GDL-II game as above, then:*

- $\mu : M \rightarrow [0,1]$ *is the probability function which, given a move, returns the probability of the move to be chosen by the player.*

The initial value of μ^0 is uniform over all the moves in a state, that is, $\mu^0(m) = \frac{1}{|M(s)|}$ for all $m \in M(s)$. Based on Definition 3 we can define for player r the mixed policy π_r with move probability μ as follow:

$$\pi_r = \{\mu(m)|r = R(s) \wedge m \in M(s)\} \tag{4}$$

Definition 4. *Let G be a GDL-II game as defined, then:*

- $\rho : S \rightarrow [0,1]$ *is the probability function which for a state returns the probability of the state to be the true state in its information set.*

ρ can be calculated with the help of the probability factor.

- $\rho Factor(s') = \rho Factor(s) * \mu(m)$
  where $s' = do(s,m)$ *and* $\rho Factor(s_0) = 1$.

With this definition we can calculate the ρ of states in an information set as follows:

$$\rho(s) = \frac{\rho Factor(s)}{\sum_{s_n \in I(s)} \rho Factor(s_n)} \tag{5}$$

We then need to calculate and assign utility values to all states in the game. The utility of each state can be calculated based on the utilities of the successor states and the probabilities of moves. The recursion will be as follow:

$$u(s) = \sum_{m \in M(s)} [u(do(s,m)) * \mu(m)] \tag{6}$$

The base cases are the utilities of terminals which are given as part of the game description.

In our ECW example, at the first iteration all $\rho Factor()$ are equal at each level. This game has a branching factor of two at all nonterminal nodes, hence $\mu^0(m) = \frac{1}{2}$ for all moves m in all states of the game. We can then calculate $\rho Factor(s_{rwt}) = \mu^0(r) * \mu^0(w) * \mu^0(t) * \rho Factor(s_0)$ which is $\frac{1}{2^3}$. As a result, the values $\rho(s_{rww})$ and $\rho(s_{bww})$ are $\frac{1}{2}$ while all the others are 1 because they all form their own singleton information set.

At the next stage, we need to calculate the value of each move in its information set and then set the move with the highest utility as the chosen one. To calculate the reward of a move we will consider all the states in the information set.

Definition 5. *Let G be a GDL-II game as defined, then:*

– *chosenMove* : $I \to M$ *is the move selection function which chooses the move with the highest reward for the player in an information set as:*

$$chosenMove(i) = argmax_m \left[\sum_{s \in i} \rho(s) * u_r(s') \right] \tag{7}$$

Here, for each s we have $s' = do(s, m)$ and $r = R(s)$. Similar legal moves in an information set have the same utility. As a result, the chosen move will be the similar move for all the states in the same information set.

In the ECW example, for the cutter the *chosenMove* in singleton information sets will be the move that leads to the highest possible utility at termination. However, for *cut red* the average utility at I_{ww} is $\rho(s_{rww}) * u(s_{rwwr}) + \rho(s_{bww}) * u(s_{bwwr})$. This is similar to the *cut blue* action at I_{ww} and equals 50. In the long run, as the game is symmetric, $\rho(s_{rww})$ and $\rho(s_{bww})$ will stay the same. So *chosenMove* switches randomly between the two moves in I_{ww}.

For the last stage, we need to update the move probability function μ as follows: Let m be *chosenMove* and m' all other moves.

$$\mu^{t+1}(m) = \frac{(\mu^t(m) * t) + 1}{t + 1} \tag{8}$$

$$\mu^{t+1}(m') = \frac{\mu^t(m') * t}{t + 1} \tag{9}$$

We will now reset all utilities for non-terminal states and $\rho Factor$ values. The iteration can be continued until the end of the pre-game calculation. In this way, we can come up with an approximation of optimal moves within a given time limit.

Coming back to the ECW example, in the long run, for the cutter's states the probability of cutting the correct wire approaches 1 except for the states in I_{ww} in which the probabilities of *cut blue* and *cut red* stay the same. As can be seen, the computational complexity of the algorithm is linear in the number of game states.

The Iterative Tree Search is summarized as Algorithm 1 below.

Algorithm 1. Iterative Tree Search

1: Generate *allInfomationSets*   ▷ using (3)
2: $t \leftarrow 0$
3: **for all** $m \in M$ **do**
4:    Initialise $\mu(m)$

5: **while** time allowed **do**
6:    **for all** $s \in S$ **do**
7:        $u(s) \leftarrow 0;\ pFactor(s) \leftarrow 0;\ \rho(s) \leftarrow 0;\ t \leftarrow t+1$
8:    $pFactor(s^0) \leftarrow 1$ ▷ s^0 is the initial state
9:    **for all** $s \in S\ \&\ m \in M(s)$ **do**
10:       $s' \leftarrow do(s, m)$
11:       $pFactor(s') \leftarrow pFactor(s) * \mu(m)$
12:    **for all** $s \in S$ **do**
13:       $\rho(s) \leftarrow \frac{pFactor(s)}{\sum_{s_n \in I(s)} pFactor(s_n)}$
14:    **for all** $s \in S\ \&\ m \in M$ **do**   ▷ For terminals, it is already set
15:       $u(s) \leftarrow u(s) + (u(do(s, m)) * \mu(m))$
16:    **for all** $i \in allInfomationSets$ **do**
17:       $chosenMove(i)$
18:       $\leftarrow \underset{m \in M(i)}{\operatorname{argmax}}[\sum_{s \in i} \rho(s) * u_{R(s)}(do(s, m))]]$
19:    **for all** $I \in allInfomationSets$ **do**
20:       $\mu(chosenMove(I)) = \frac{(\mu(chosenMove(I)) \times t) + 1}{t+1}$
21:       **for all** $m \in M(I)\ \&\ m \neq chosenMove(i)$ **do**
22:          $\mu(m) = \frac{\mu(m) \times t}{t+1}$

---

4   Analysis

In the following, we characterize the classes of GDL-II games that our ITS can solve. We will resort to the theory of fictitious play to this end. We also demonstrate how HP-II fails in these games and show experimental results to confirm our observations. All mentioned games have either been previously introduced in the literature or are extensions of games from the literature.

4.1   Games with Dominant Pure Strategy and Single Player Games

ITS can correctly solve games in which there exists a dominant pure strategy. Having a dominant strategy means playing one specific move at each information set guarantees the player the highest reward. Also, it means that the actions of the opponents will not affect the decision of the player. If a single-player game with incomplete information has an optimal strategy, then this will be a pure dominant strategy, as the random player has no intention of changing its strategy.

The ITS algorithm at the first iteration assigns equal probabilities to all moves from the same information set. This means that no $\mu(m)$ will ever have zero probability. As the calculation progresses, the player with a dominant strategy tends to play more of it because states on the path of a dominant strategy have the highest rewards and the probability of the parent state never changes. As a result, the probability of playing a dominant strategy increases with each iteration. So $\rho(s) * u_r(s')$ always increases and will always be the chosen move. We can use the ECW game to illustrate how ITS can correctly play this type of games and also why HP-II fails.

Example: Extended Cutting Wire. The game was inspired by the "cutting wire" game originally published to motivate the HP-II technique [18]. In the original version, the teller can *tell* or *wait* only once. HP uses complete-information sampling and therefore fails to solve this problem (since information gains can have no value), but HP-II successfully solves the original version of the game. We have extended the cutting wire in order to show that ITS can correctly value information in deeper parts of the game tree while HP-II is "short-sighted" in this regard. ITS correctly chooses to *tell* at the second level, where it is less costly, while the HP-II player chooses to *tell* at the first level because of its short-sightedness when valuing information.

HP-II uses nested players to overcome the limitations of model sampling as used in HP. However, at each step it sees information-gathering moves only one level ahead. This causes the algorithm to choose *tell1* and *wait2* rather than *wait1* and *tell2*. More precisely, the move selection policy of HP-II π_{hpii} can be described as:

$$argmax_{m \in M(s)} \left[\sum_{s' \in I(s)} eval(replay(s_0, I_{r \in R}(do(s', m))), \pi_{hp}), \pi_{hp}, n) \right] \quad (10)$$

We have modified the algorithm to suit sequential games.[3] At state s_r, π_{hpii} chooses the move based on which of $\pi_{hp}(s_{rw})$ or $\pi_{hp}(s_{rt})$ gives the higher expected reward. The HP-II policy, π_{hp}, uses a Monte-Carlo search, so the move *wait1* returns $\frac{100+90}{2}$ and move *tell1* returns $\frac{70+80}{2}$. As a result, HP-II considers *tell1* a better move than *wait1*. We refer to this problem as *short-sighted information valuation*.

Our new ITS algorithm can correctly value the information anywhere in the game tree. To illustrate this, recall the explanation for HP-II. As previously described, for the *arm red* part of the game tree, the cutter's utilities in the long run will be: $u(s_{rtt}) = 70$, $u(s_{rtw}) = 80$, $u(s_{rwt}) = 90$ and $u(s_{rww}) = 50$. Then using Eqs. (7) and (6) we obtain $u(s_{rw}) = 90$ and $u(s_{rt}) = 80$. As a result, the *chosenMove*$(I(s_r))$ will be *wait1*. Analogously, we can show that *chosenMove*$(I(s_b))$ is *wait1* too.

---

[3] The *replay* function replays from the initial state to the given state. In the sequential ECW game, where the only information set belongs to the *secondPlayer*, the *replay* function will be reduced to a simple information set function.

To validate our claims we have run ITS with the extended cutting wire game. The graph in Fig. 2 shows the probability of the *tell* move at the two different stages of the game during the first 1,000 iterations. If the probability of the telling action is high in any state, then the probability of waiting is low and vice versa. As can be seen from the graph, the probability of choosing the telling action twice quickly converges to zero at early iterations. The probability of the first, more costly telling move also drops to almost zero in less than 1,000 iterations. In fact, after less than 200 iterations ITS will very likely choose to wait first and then to tell.

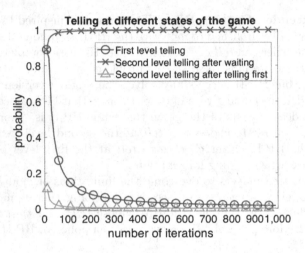

Fig. 2. Probability of *tell* at different states during the first 1,000 iterations in the extended cutting wire game.

4.2 Non-locality Problem

Frank and Basin [5] have formalized and analyzed the problem of *non-locality*. Non-locality happens when an algorithm only considers children of a state to find the best move for that state. Our ITS algorithm models the opponent, which can be shown to lessen the impact of this problem.[4]

Example: The Game in Fig. 5 [6]. To show the ability of ITS algorithm to solve games that exhibit the non-locality problem, we consider the motivating example from [5]. In this game, the first move by random is only visible to the *secondPlayer* while players' moves are visible to each other. The random choice places the game in a particular world, and the utilities for the players depend on

---

[4] Frank and Basin [7] have introduced the "Vector MiniMax" technique, which also just lessens, rather than completely avoids, the impact of non-locality.

their moves and the world they are in.[5] Figure 3 depicts the game tree for this game and shows *firstPlayer*'s optimal strategy. This strategy guarantees that the first player always receives 1 in w_1. ITS is able to always play correctly at states a and e from the first iteration on because these are the dominant moves. Figure 4 shows the mixed strategy of the player at state d after 100 iterations. After less than 100 iterations, our implemented ITS was also able to play left at d with a probability of 99%.

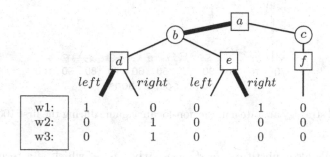

Fig. 3. Game with non-locality problem represented in world model.

4.3   One-Step Joint-Move Two-Player Zero-Sum Games

We show that ITS reduces to fictitious play for this category of games, and since fictitious play is known to solve these games, ITS can solve them too. For ITS we convert this category of games into a two-step sequential game with incomplete information. All moves of the *firstPlayer* lead to states that are all in the same information set. To show that the ITS algorithm works similar to fictitious play for this class of games, we will show that the updating policy and the move selection of fictitious play is similar to ITS. We refer to the player who moves first as the *firstPlayer* and call the opponent the *secondPlayer*. For both players, updating the mixed policy π via Eq. (1) is identical to updating μ of moves in ITS, that is, Eqs. (8) and (9).

For the move selection policy of ITS we need to consider each player separately. With regard to choosing the best move for the *firstPlayer* in ITS, if we combine Eqs. (7) and (6), then for *chosenMove*() we will get:

$$argmax_{m_1} \left[\sum_{s \in i} \rho(s) * \sum_{m_2 \in M(s')} [u(do(s', m_2) * \mu(m_2))] \right] \quad (11)$$

Here, s is the initial state s_0 and is in a singleton information set; s' is the state after the initial state, referred to as s_{m1} in what follows. $\rho(s_0)$ is always

---

[5] This game can, of course, be straightforwardly axiomatized in GDL-II as a GGP-II game [22].

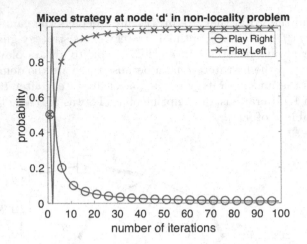

Fig. 4. Mixed strategy at state d in the non-locality game during the first 100 iterations.

equal to 1. We also substitute $do(s', m_2)$ with s_{m1m2}, which is a terminal state with a fixed reward. Also, to simplify notation, we replace $M(s')$ with M_2. For $chosenMove()$ we then obtain the following:

$$argmax_{m1}\left[\sum_{m2 \in M_2} [u(s_{m1m2} * \mu(m_2))] \right] \tag{12}$$

Considering the relation of mixed move policy and mixed policy described in Eq. (4), this equation is indeed equal to the best respond Eq. (2) for fictitious play.

With regard to choosing the best move for the *secondPlayer* in ITS, the action of the *firstPlayer* changes the probability of state $\rho(s)$. Since the *secondPlayer*'s decision states are all in the same information set and are all generated from the initial state, $\rho Factor(s_{m1}) = \mu(m1)$. So $\rho(s_{m1}) = \frac{\mu(m1)}{\sum_{m \in M_2} \mu(m)}$. By definition the denominator is equal to 1. By substituting these in Eq. (7), for $chosenMove()$ we obtain:

$$argmax_{m2 \in M_2}\left[\sum_{m1 \in M_1} \mu(m1) * u(s_{m1m2}) \right] \tag{13}$$

which is identical to Eq. (12) with $m1$ being replaced by $m2$. This completes the proof that ITS reduces to basic fictitious play for this category of the games and that, therefore, ITS is able to correctly play any one-step, joint-move zero-sum game with two players. As an example, we look at Biased Penalty Kick, which is a common game in game theory to show the ability of an algorithm to find a Nash equilibrium (NE).

Example: Biased Penalty Kick. This is a well-known game to illustrate opponent modeling and the value of playing a mixed strategy: If the kicker shoots right and the keeper catches, the keeper gets 60; otherwise, the kicker gets 60. If the kicker shoots left the rewards will instead be 40. There is no pure NE, and the optimal mixed strategy in a NE for the kicker is to shoot 40% right and 60% left. For the goalkeeper, it is jumping 40% to the left and 60% to the right.

While both HP and HP-II only deliver pure strategies, ITS can solve this problem after just a few iterations as this game is a one-step joint-move game. To verify this claim we have run our implemented ITS algorithm on this problem. Figure 5 shows the mixed strategy of the goalkeeper for the first 10,000 iterations. ITS quickly finds the correct probabilities for both players.

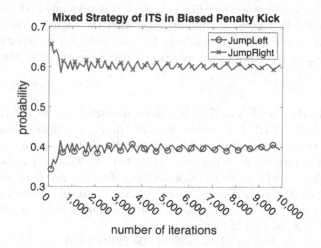

Fig. 5. Mixed strategy of the goal keeper for the biased penalty kick game for the first 10,000 iterations.

4.4 Move Separable Games

In this category of games, each player is only responsible for moves in one stage of the game. This means that when the *secondPlayer* begins to move after a series of moves by the *firstPlayer*, then after the *secondPlayer* has made their moves the game ends, and also the *firstPlayer* cannot interrupt the *secondPlayer*'s course of actions. If the random player exists in the game, its actions are visible to the player of the corresponding stage of the game. In this class of games, the *secondPlayer* may or may not be able to see some or all of the actions performed by the *firstPlayer*. We will show that these games will be reduced to a game where the *firstPlayer* chooses a joint-move game for both players to play. HP-II fails to solve games in this class as it can only find a pure strategy, whereas again the ITS algorithm can solve this category of games.

First, consider the simpler case of games where the *secondPlayer* cannot see the *firstPlayer*'s moves. The probability of a state to be the true state in the information set of the *secondPlayer* depends on the sequence of the *firstPlayer*'s moves. This sequence can be considered as one single, combined move, whose probability is the same as the frequency with which the corresponding sequence is chosen. The game can therefore obviously be reduced to a one-step, joint-move game that is solvable by the ITS algorithm.

Now consider the case when the *secondPlayer* can see some of the actions of the *firstPlayer*. The *firstPlayer* can lead the *secondPlayer* into one of possible information sets. The $\rho(s)$ of the states in each information set can be changed by the unobserved moves of the *firstPlayer*. Thus a game of this type can be reduced to a game where the *firstPlayer* chooses a subgame of a one-step, joint-move game with the highest NE payout for himself among all subgames and then play the subgame corresponding to the NE strategy. As described in the previous section, ITS can solve this subgame and determine the payout for each NE. Choosing the subgame with the highest NE payout then just requires a simple search. In this way ITS can solve Move Separable Games. We end our analysis with an example of a game from the literature that falls into this category.

Example: Banker and Thief. This game was used in the HP-II paper [18] to show the ability of HP-II to value the withholding of information. There are two banks in this game, one of which has a faulty alarm system. The owner of the bank that is faulty has to decide to distribute $100 between the two banks in $10 notes. The thief can see the distribution of the money between the banks but not which of the two is faulty. If the thief decides to rob the faulty bank then he succeeds in getting the money, otherwise the banker receives all the money left in his bank at the end of the game.

Using HP-II, the banker places $40 in the faulty bank and $60 in the other, implicitly making the assumption that the thief is greedy and will choose to rob the bank with $60, which means the banker wins. This strategy was considered as the winning strategy in HP-II paper [18]. We claim that this is, in fact, a suboptimal strategy as the banker wrongly assumes the thief to be greedy. Indeed, the thief might well assume the banker to assume that he is greedy, and hence he will decide to go after the $40. The best strategy for this game must, therefore, be a mixed strategy so that the thief becomes indifferent to choosing a bank. Only then is the (mixed) strategy a Nash equilibrium. Different distributions lead to different NE with different expected payout. The highest expected payout for the banker is a $50-$50 distribution with an expected payout of $25, while the expected payout for the $40-$60 distribution is just $24. Since this is a Move Separable Game, ITS can solve it in contrast to HP-II.

To prove our claim, we have run our ITS algorithm with this game, but to make it more challenging we added two extra safe banks. The banker can then choose a distribution of his money in $10-chunks among four banks. There is a total of 287 ways to do so. Table 1 shows the probabilities for some mixed strategies for the banker in the case when the first bank has been selected as faulty by the random player. The theoretical analysis for this variant of the game shows that the optimal strategy is to put $50 in a faulty and $50 in any of the safe banks. As can be seen from the table, this is what the ITS algorithm will do in 94% of the times after one million iterations. Figure 6 shows how the probabilities for some of the 287 strategies evolve.

Table 1. Probability of choosing a money distribution by ITS in the banker and thief game.

Money distribution	50 50 0 0	50 0 50 0	50 0 0 50	0 50 50 0	all others
Probability of choosing	35.67%	27.5%	30.88%	0%	5.95%

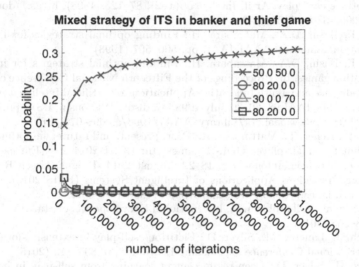

Fig. 6. The probability change toward equilibrium for four strategies in the banker and thief game when the faulty bank is the first one.

5   Conclusion

We have introduced the Iterative Tree Search (ITS) algorithm as a significant improvement over state-of-the-art algorithms, in particular HP-II, for general game playing with incomplete information. While HP-II is short-sighted on valuing information, our ITS algorithm has been shown to correctly value information in a game by gathering information at the lowest possible cost that promises the highest benefit. An ITS-based general game player is also able to withhold information from opponents and to play a NE on a number of classes of games. Moreover, HP-II is not able to compute mixed strategies, so it fails to find the best strategy in games that require opponent modeling. With ITS we can overcome these limitations by iteratively self-playing the game using an incomplete-information tree and thus learn the expected behavior of a rational opponent.

References

1. Brown, G.W.: Iterative solution of games by fictitious play. Activity Anal. Prod. Allocation **13**(1), 374–376 (1951)
2. Cowling, P.I., Powley, E.J., Whitehouse, D.: Information set monte carlo tree search. IEEE Trans. Comput. Intell. AI Games **4**(2), 120–143 (2012)
3. Edelkamp, S., Federholzner, T., Kissmann, P.: Searching with partial belief states in general games with incomplete information. In: Glimm, B., Krüger, A. (eds.) KI 2012. LNCS (LNAI), vol. 7526, pp. 25–36. Springer, Heidelberg (2012). https://doi.org/10.1007/978-3-642-33347-7_3
4. Frank, I., Basin, D.: A theoretical and empirical investigation of search in imperfect information games. Theor. Comput. Sci. **252**(1–2), 217–256 (2001)
5. Frank, I., Basin, D.A.: Search in games with incomplete information: a case study using bridge card play. Artif. Intell. **100**(1–2), 87–123 (1998). https://doi.org/10.1016/S0004-3702(97)00082-9
6. Frank, I., Basin, D.A., Matsubara, H.: Finding optimal strategies for imperfect information games. In: AAAI/IAAI, pp. 500–507 (1998)
7. Frank, I., Basin, D.A., Matsubara, H.: Finding optimal strategies for imperfect information games. In: Proceedings of the Fifteenth National Conference on Artificial Intelligence and Tenth Innovative Applications of Artificial Intelligence Conference, AAAI 98, IAAI 98, 26–30 July 1998, Madison, Wisconsin, USA, pp. 500–507 (1998). http://www.aaai.org/Library/AAAI/1998/aaai98-071.php
8. Geißer, F., Keller, T., Mattmüller, R.: Past, present, and future: an optimal online algorithm for single-player GDL-II games. In: ECAI 2014–21st European Conference on Artificial Intelligence, 18–22 August 2014, Prague, Czech Republic - Including Prestigious Applications of Intelligent Systems (PAIS 2014), pp. 357–362 (2014). https://doi.org/10.3233/978-1-61499-419-0-357,
9. Gill, R.: Monty hall problem. In: International Encyclopaedia of Statistical Science, pp. 858–863 (2010)
10. Heinrich, J., Lanctot, M., Silver, D.: Fictitious self-play in extensive-form games. In: International Conference on Machine Learning, pp. 805–813 (2015)
11. Heinrich, J., Silver, D.: Deep reinforcement learning from self-play in imperfect-information games. CoRR abs/1603.01121 (2016)/. http://arxiv.org/abs/1603.01121
12. Johanson, M.B.: Robust strategies and counter-strategies: building a champion level computer poker player. Masters Abstracts Int. **46** (2007)
13. Long, J.R., Sturtevant, N.R., Buro, M., Furtak, T.: Understanding the success of perfect information monte carlo sampling in game tree search. In: AAAI (2010)
14. Love, N., Hinrichs, T., Haley, D., Schkufza, E., Genesereth, M.: General game playing: game description language specification (2008)
15. Monderer, D., Shapley, L.S.: Potential games. Games Econ. Behav. **14**(1), 124–143 (1996)
16. Romstad, T., Costalba, M., Kiiski, J., et al.: Stockfish: a strong open source chess engine. https://stockfishchess.org/. Accessed 1 May 2018
17. Schofield, M.J., Cerexhe, T.J., Thielscher, M.: Hyperplay: a solution to general game playing with imperfect information. In: AAAI. Citeseer (2012)
18. Schofield, M.J., Thielscher, M.: Lifting model sampling for general game playing to incomplete-information models. In: AAAI, pp. 3585–3591 (2015)
19. Schofield, M.J., Thielscher, M.: The scalability of the hyperplay technique for imperfect-information games. In: AAAI Workshop: Computer Poker and Imperfect Information Games (2016)

20. Silver, D., et al.: Mastering chess and shogi by self-play with a general reinforcement learning algorithm. arXiv preprint arXiv:1712.01815 (2017)
21. Thielscher, M.: A general game description language for incomplete information games. In: AAAI, vol. 10, pp. 994–999. Citeseer (2010)
22. Thielscher, M.: The general game playing description language is universal, Barcelona, pp. 1107–1112, July 2011
23. Zinkevich, M., Johanson, M., Bowling, M., Piccione, C.: Regret minimization in games with incomplete information. In: Advances in Neural Information Processing Systems, pp. 1729–1736 (2008)

Machine Learning and Monte Carlo Tree Search

Spatial Average Pooling for Computer Go

Tristan Cazenave[(✉)]

Université Paris-Dauphine, PSL Research University, CNRS, LAMSADE,
Paris, France
Tristan.Cazenave@dauphine.fr

Abstract. Computer Go has improved up to a superhuman level thanks
to Monte Carlo Tree Search (MCTS) combined with Deep Learning. The
best computer Go programs use reinforcement learning to train a policy
and a value network. These networks are used in a MCTS algorithm to
provide strong computer Go players. In this paper we propose to improve
the architecture of a value network using Spatial Average Pooling.

1 Introduction

Monte Carlo Tree Search (MCTS) has been successfully applied to many games
and problems [1]. The most popular MCTS algorithm is Upper Confidence
bounds for Trees (UCT) [9]. MCTS is particularly successful in games [8]. A
variant of UCT when priors are available is PUCT [11]. AlphaGo [12] uses a
variant of PUCT as its MCTS algorithm. AlphaGo Zero [14] and AlphaZero [13]
also use PUCT as their MCTS algorithm. Golois, our computer Go player, uses
as its MCTS algorithm the same variant of PUCT as AlphaGo.

AlphaGo uses a policy network to bias the choice of moves to be tried in the
tree descent, and a value network to evaluate the leaves of the tree. In AlphaGo
Zero, the evaluation of a leaf is uniquely due to the value network and playouts
are not used anymore. Moreover the policy and value network are contained in
the same neural network that has two heads, one for the policy and one for the
value.

AlphaGo and AlphaGo Zero were applied to the game of Go. The approach
has been extended to chess and Shogi with AlphaZero [13]. After a few hours
of self play and training with 5 000 Tensor Processing Units from Google, AlphaZero was able to defeat top Chess and Shogi programs (Stockfish and Elmo)
using a totally different approach than these programs. AlphaZero uses 1,000
times fewer evaluations than Stockfish and Elmo for the same thinking time. It
uses PUCT instead of AlphaBeta and a combined value and policy network.

The AlphaGo Zero approach has been replicated by many researchers. The
Leela Zero program is a community effort to replicate the AlphaGo Zero experiments. People donate their GPU time to make Leela Zero play self-play games
[10]. The networks trained on self play games are then tested against the current

Electronic supplementary material The online version of this chapter (https://
doi.org/10.1007/978-3-030-24337-1_6) contains supplementary material, which is available to authorized users.

© Springer Nature Switzerland AG 2019
T. Cazenave et al. (Eds.): CGW 2018, CCIS 1017, pp. 119–126, 2019.
https://doi.org/10.1007/978-3-030-24337-1_6

best network and replace it if the result of the match is meaningful enough. The best network is then used for randomized self-play. Most of the computing time used by programs replicating the AlphaGo Zero approach is spent in self-play.

The ELF framework from Facebook AI Research [15] is an open source initiative to implement reinforcement algorithms for games. It has been applied to the game of Go following the AlphaGo Zero approach [16]. The resulting ELF Go program running on a single V100 GPU has beaten top Korean professionals Go players 14 to 0 and Leela Zero 200 to 0. It was trained for two weeks using 2 000 GPUs. It is a strong superhuman level computer Go player, however it has the same kind of weaknesses as Leela Zero and other Zero bots: it sometimes plays a ladder that is not working and loses the game because of this ladder problem.

Another partially open source Go program is Phoenix Go by Tencent [20]. It won the last computer Go tournament at Fuzhou, China in April 2018 defeating FineArt and LeelaZero.

In this paper we are interested in improving a value network for Golois our computer Go program. We have previously shown that residual networks can improve a policy network [2,3]. We also use residual networks for our value network which is trained on self-play games of the policy network. We propose to improve on the standard residual value network adding Spatial Average Pooling layers to the usual residual value network. Our experiments are performed using Golois with and without Spatial Average Pooling. The AQ open source Go program [19] also uses Spatial Average Pooling in its value network.

We now give the outline of the paper. The next section outlines the training of a value network. The third section details the PUCT search algorithm. The fourth section explains Spatial Average Pooling. The fifth section gives experimental results. The last section concludes.

2   Training a Value Network

Training of the value network uses games self-played by the policy network. Golois policy network has a KGS 4 dan level using residual networks and three output planes [2,3,17].

The playing policy is randomized, Golois chooses a move randomly between the moves advised by the policy network that have a probability of being the best move greater than the probability of the best move minus 0.2. This policy enable sufficient randomization while retaining a good level of play. This is the randomization strategy that was used to make Golois policy network play on KGS.

The architecture of the policy network uses nine residual blocks an three output planes, one for each of the three next moves of the game. The network was trained on games between professional players played between 1900 and 2015.

The architecture of our first value network is also based on residual networks and has nine residual blocks. The first layer of the network is a convolutional layer with 1×1 filters that takes the 47 input planes and transform them into 256 19×19 planes. The last layers of the network are a 1×1 convolution layer that converse the 256 planes to a single plane, the single plane is then reshaped into a one dimensional tensor and followed by two completely connected layers.

In order to be able to play handicap games, Golois uses nine outputs for its value network. One output for each possible final score of a self-play game between 180.0 and 189.0. The final score is the score of the Black player. All output neurons representing a score greater than the score of the self-played game are set to one during training and all neurons strictly smaller are set to zero. For example if the score of a game is 183.0, the first three outputs are set to zero and the next six outputs are set to one.

When using the value network for a game, the corresponding neuron is used for the evaluation of states. If the game is even and the komi is 7.5 the neuron for a score greater than 184.0 is used, if the game is handicap one and the komi is 0.5 the neuron for a score greater than 180.0 is used. Using multiple outputs for the value network has also been used independently for the CGI Go program [18].

3   PUCT

In order to be complete, the PUCT algorithm is given in Algorithm 1. Lines 2–5 deals with getting the possible moves and stopping if the board is terminal. Line 6 gets the entry of the board in the transposition table. Each board is associated to a Zobrist hash code that enables to calculate the index of the board in the transposition table. An entry in the transposition table contains the total number of playouts that have gone through the state, the mean of all the evaluations of the children of the node and of the node itself, the number of playouts for each possible moves, and the prior for each possible move given by the policy network. The policy network uses a softmax activation for the output of the network, so the priors given by the policy network can be considered as probabilities of each move being the best. Lines 7–23 are executed when the state has already been seen and is present in the transposition table. The goal is to find the move that maximizes the PUCT formula. The PUCT formula is:

$$argmax_m(mean_m + c \times prior_m \times \frac{\sqrt{t}}{p_m})$$

with c being the PUCT constant, $prior_m$ being the probability for move m given by the policy network, t being the sum of the number of playouts that have gone through the node and p_m being the number of playouts that start with move m.

On line 20 the move that maximizes the PUCT formula is played, then the recursive call to PUCT is done online 22 for the selected child of the current node. When PUCT returns from the call and gets the evaluation of the new leaf, it updates the values of the current node with the result of the search on line 23. This means it increases by one the total number of playouts of the node, it increases by one the playouts of move m and updates the mean of move m with res.

Lines 25–27 are executed when the state is not part of the PUCT tree. In this case it adds an entry in the transposition table for this state and gets the evaluation of the board from the value network. We use MCTS without playouts. The leaves are evaluated by the value network alone. The value network is run

on the eight symmetrical boards of the state to evaluate, and the average of the
eight evaluations is the evaluation of the leaf.

Algorithm 1. The PUCT algorithm.

1: PUCT (*board*, *player*)
2:     *moves* ← possible moves on *board*
3:     **if** *board* is terminal **then**
4:         **return** evaluation (*board*)
5:     **end if**
6:     *t* ← entry of *board* in the transposition table
7:     **if** *t* exists **then**
8:         *bestValue* ← −∞
9:         **for** *m* in *moves* **do**
10:             *t* ← *t.totalPlayouts*
11:             *mean* ← *t.mean*[*m*]
12:             *p* ← *t.playouts*[*m*]
13:             *prior* ← *t.prior*[*m*]
14:             *value* ← *mean* + *c* × *prior* × $\frac{\sqrt{t}}{p}$
15:             **if** *value* > *bestValue* **then**
16:                 *bestValue* ← *value*
17:                 *bestMove* ← *m*
18:             **end if**
19:         **end for**
20:         play (*board*, *bestMove*)
21:         *player* ← opponent (*player*)
22:         *res* ← PUCT (*board*, *player*)
23:         update *t* with *res*
24:     **else**
25:         *t* ← new entry of *board* in the transposition table
26:         *res* ← evaluation (*board*, *player*)
27:         update *t*
28:     **end if**
29:     **return** *res*

We use tree parallelism for the PUCT search of Golois. Twelve threads are
running in parallel and share the same tree. Each thread is assigned to one of
the four GPUs and calls the forward pass of the policy and value networks on
this GPU.

We have also found that it improves the number of nodes per second to use a
minibatch greater than 8. The standard algorithm uses minibatch of size 8 since
there are eight symmetrical states for a leaf of the tree. However current GPUs
can be used more efficiently with larger minibatches. The best results we had
were with minibatches of size 16. We only get the value of leaf every two leaves.
It means that after the first call to PUCT, a second tree descent is performed
to get a second leaf to evaluate corresponding to 8 more states. The second tree
descent does not usually find the same leaf as the first tree descent since during

each tree descent a virtual loss is added to the number of playouts of the selected move. This ensures that the further tree descents do not always select the same moves. So after the second descent, both the first leaf and the second leaf are evaluated, with 8 symmetrical states each, resulting in a minibatch of 16 states.

4   Spatial Average Pooling

Spatial Average Pooling takes the average of a rectangle of cells of the input matrix as the output of the layer. Table 1 illustrates the application of a 2 × 2 Spatial Average Pooling on a 4 × 4 matrix. The elements of the 4 × 4 matrix are split into four 2 × 2 matrices and each 2 × 2 matrix is averaged to give each element of an output 2 × 2 matrix.

Table 1. Spatial average pooling.

8 3	4 7
4 1	6 3
2 6	3 9
1 7	2 6

4	5
4	5

We used Spatial Average Pooling in the last layers of Golois value network with a size 2 × 2 and a stride of 2 as in the Table 1 example.

When applying Spatial Average Pooling with a size 2 × 2 and a stride of 2 to 19 × 19 planes, we add a padding of one around the 19 × 19 plane. Therefore the resulting planes are 10 × 10 planes. When applying Spatial Average Pooling again to the 10 × 10 planes with a padding of one we obtain 6 × 6 planes. The last convolutional layer of the value network is a single 6 × 6 plane. It is flattened to give a vector of 36 neurons. It is then followed by a 50 neurons layer and the final 9 neurons output followed by a Sigmoid (the value network outputs the probability of winning between 0 and 1).

The Spatial Average Pooling is meaningful for a value network since such a networks outputs a winning probability that is related to the estimated score of the board. If neurons in the various planes represent the probability of an intersection to be Black territory in the end, averaging such probabilities gives the winning probability. So using Spatial Average Pooling layers can push the value network to represent probabilities of ownership for the different parts of the board and help the training process.

In AlphaGo Zero [14], policy and value networks share the same weights of a network with two different heads. One head for the policy network and one head for the value network. Our improvement of the value network can still be used in such an architecture, using Spatial Average Pooling for the value head.

5   Experimental Results

Experiments make PUCT with a given network play against PUCT with another network. 200 games are played between algorithms in order to evaluate them. Each move of each game is allocated 0.5 seconds on a four GPU machine with 6 threads. This enables to play between 40 and 80 tree descents per move. In all experiments we use a PUCT constant of 0.3 which is the best we found.

The experiments were done using the Torch framework [7], combining C++ code for the PUCT search with lua/Torch code for the forward passes of the networks as well as for the training of the value networks. The minibatches are created on the fly with C++ code that randomly chooses states of the self played games and combine them in a size 50 minibatch. Each state is associated to the result of the self played game. Once the minibatch is ready it is passed to the lua code that deals with the computation of the loss and the Stochastic Gradient Descent. We use the same 1,600,000 self played games for training the value networks.

The value network including Spatial Average Pooling has 128 planes for each layer. It starts with six residual blocks then applies Spatial Average Pooling, followed by three residual blocks then another Spatial Average Pooling, followed by three other residual blocks. The two fully connected layers of 50 and 9 neurons complete the network. This value network is named SAP (6,3,3) in Table 2.

The competing value network is the standard residual value network used in Golois. It has nine residual blocks with 256 planes per layer. It is named α (9,256) in Table 2. Deeper residual value networks were trained for Golois without giving much better results, that is why we kept the nine blocks value network. The original AlphaGo used 13 layers convolutional networks while AlphaGo Zero uses either 20 or 40 residual blocks with 256 planes. Our self-play data is not as high level as the self-play data of AlphaGo Zero. That may explain why deeper networks make little difference.

Table 2 gives the evolution of the training losses of the two networks with the number of epochs. One epoch is defined as 5 000 000 training examples. The minibatch size is 50, so an epoch is composed of 100,000 training steps. We can see in Table 2 that SAP (6,3,3) starts training with a smaller loss than α (9,256), but that eventually the losses are close after 63 epochs.

Table 2. Evolution of the training loss of the value networks.

Epochs	1	3	7	15	31	63
α (9,256)	677	560	532	522	516	510
SAP (6,3,3)	654	554	530	521	515	511

We made the SAP (6,3,3) value network play fast games against the α (9,256) value network. Both networks use the same policy network to evaluate priors and the parameters of the PUCT search such as the PUCT constant were tuned for the α (9,256) value network. We found that a small PUCT constant of 0.3 is best, this may be due to the quality of the policy network that implies less exploration and more confidence in the value network since it directs the exploration toward the good moves.

SAP (6,3,3) wins 70.0% of the time against the usual residual value network. The size of the network file for SAP (6,3,3) is 28,530,177 while the size of the network file for α (9,256) is 85,954,310. The training time for 100 minibatches is 6.0 seconds for SAP (6,3,3) while the training time for 100 minibatches is 12.5 seconds for α (9,256).

Using this network, Golois reached an 8d level on the KGS Go server running on a 4 GPU machine with approximately 2 500 tree descents and 9 seconds thinking time per move.

6   Conclusion

We have proposed the use of Spatial Average Pooling to improve a value network for the game of Go. The value network using Spatial Average Pooling is much smaller than the usual residual value network and has better results.

We have also detailed our parallel PUCT algorithm that makes use of the GPU power by making forward passes on minibatches of states instead of a single state.

The value network we have trained has multiple output neurons instead of one as in usual networks It enables it to be used with different komi values and therefore to play handicap games correctly. It is important for game play on servers such as KGS where due to its 8d strength it plays handicap games most of the time.

In future work we plan to use Spatial Average Pooling for the value head of a combined value/policy network. We also plan to improve the search algorithm and its parallelization [4–6].

References

1. Browne, C., et al.: A survey of Monte Carlo tree search methods. IEEE TCIAIG **4**(1), 1–43 (2012)
2. Cazenave, T.: Improved policy networks for computer go. In: Winands, M.H.M., van den Herik, H.J., Kosters, W.A. (eds.) ACG 2017. LNCS, vol. 10664, pp. 90–100. Springer, Cham (2017). https://doi.org/10.1007/978-3-319-71649-7_8
3. Cazenave, T.: Residual networks for computer go. IEEE Trans. Games **10**(1), 107–110 (2018)
4. Cazenave, T., Jouandeau, N.: On the parallelization of UCT. In: Proceedings of the Computer Games Workshop, pp. 93–101. Citeseer (2007)
5. Cazenave, T., Jouandeau, N.: A parallel Monte-Carlo tree search algorithm. In: van den Herik, H.J., Xu, X., Ma, Z., Winands, M.H.M. (eds.) CG 2008. LNCS, vol. 5131, pp. 72–80. Springer, Heidelberg (2008). https://doi.org/10.1007/978-3-540-87608-3_7

6. Chaslot, G.M.J.-B., Winands, M.H.M., van den Herik, H.J.: Parallel Monte-Carlo tree search. In: van den Herik, H.J., Xu, X., Ma, Z., Winands, M.H.M. (eds.) CG 2008. LNCS, vol. 5131, pp. 60–71. Springer, Heidelberg (2008). https://doi.org/10.1007/978-3-540-87608-3_6

7. Collobert, R., Kavukcuoglu, K., Farabet, C.: Torch7: a matlab-like environment for machine learning. In: BigLearn, NIPS Workshop, number EPFL-CONF-192376 (2011)

8. Coulom, R.: Efficient selectivity and backup operators in Monte-Carlo tree search. In: van den Herik, H.J., Ciancarini, P., Donkers, H.H.L.M.J. (eds.) CG 2006. LNCS, vol. 4630, pp. 72–83. Springer, Heidelberg (2007). https://doi.org/10.1007/978-3-540-75538-8_7

9. Kocsis, L., Szepesvári, C.: Bandit based Monte-Carlo planning. In: Fürnkranz, J., Scheffer, T., Spiliopoulou, M. (eds.) ECML 2006. LNCS (LNAI), vol. 4212, pp. 282–293. Springer, Heidelberg (2006). https://doi.org/10.1007/11871842_29

10. Pascutto, G.-C.: Leela zero (2018). http://zero.sjeng.org/

11. Rosin, C.D.: Multi-armed bandits with episode context. Ann. Math. Artif. Intell. **61**(3), 203–230 (2011)

12. Silver, D., et al.: Mastering the game of go with deep neural networks and tree search. Nature **529**(7587), 484–489 (2016)

13. Silver, D., et al.: Mastering chess and Shogi by self-play with a general reinforcement learning algorithm. arXiv preprint arXiv:1712.01815 (2017)

14. Silver, D., et al.: Mastering the game of go without human knowledge. Nature **550**(7676), 354 (2017)

15. Tian, Y., Gong, Q., Shang, W., Wu, Y., Zitnick, C.L.: Elf: an extensive, lightweight and flexible research platform for real-time strategy games. In: Advances in Neural Information Processing Systems, pp. 2656–2666 (2017)

16. Tian, Y., Ma, J., Gong, Q., Sengupta, S., Chen, Z., Zitnick, C.L.: ELF OpenGo (2018). https://github.com/pytorch/ELF

17. Tian, Y., Zhu, Y.: Better computer go player with neural network and long-term prediction. In: ICLR (2016)

18. Wu, T.-R., et al.: Multi-labelled value networks for computer go. arXiv e-prints, May 2017

19. Yamaguchi, Y.: AQ (2018). https://github.com/ymgaq/AQ

20. Zeng, Q., Zhang, J., Zeng, Z., Li, Y., Chen, M., Liu, S.: Phoenixgo (2018). https://github.com/Tencent/PhoenixGo

Analyzing the Impact of Knowledge and Search in Monte Carlo Tree Search in Go

Farhad Haqiqat[✉] and Martin Müller[✉]

University of Alberta, Edmonton, AB T6G 2R3, Canada
{haqiqath,mmueller}@ualberta.ca

Abstract. Domain-specific knowledge plays a significant role in the success of many Monte Carlo Tree Search (MCTS) programs. The details of how knowledge affects MCTS are still not well understood. In this paper, we focus on identifying the effects of different types of knowledge on the behaviour of the Monte Carlo Tree Search algorithm, using the game of Go as a case study. We measure the performance of each type of knowledge, and of deeper search by using two main metrics: The move prediction rate on games played by professional players, and the playing strength of an implementation in the open source program Fuego. We compare the result of these two evaluation methods in detail, in order to understand how effective they are in fully understanding a program's behaviour. A feature-based approach refines our analysis tools, and addresses some of the shortcomings of these two evaluation methods. This approach allows us to interpret different components of knowledge and deeper search in different phases of a game, and helps us to obtain a deeper understanding of the role of knowledge and its relation with search in the MCTS algorithm.

Keywords: MCTS · Go · Knowledge · Evaluation · Features

1 Introduction

Go programs achieved success first on small boards due to the power of Monte Carlo Tree Search, and later on the full 19×19 board due to the power of knowledge encoded in the deep neural networks. The MCTS based program Fuego [1] was the first program able to beat a top human professional player in Go on a 9×9 size board in 2008 [8]. Fuego achieved this level of play by using a MCTS algorithm enhanced by simple knowledge of features and patterns. Despite the successes that programs had on the 9×9 size board, the full 19×19 size board remained out of reach until recently, when AlphaGo [17,18] far exceeded the human level of play. AlphaGo uses a variant of MCTS with a very strong knowledge obtained through learning with Neural Networks (NN) in order to improve the search in MCTS.

Many studies have focused on increasing the strength of knowledge and methods of incorporating knowledge in MCTS based programs [4–6,16,20]. In order

© Springer Nature Switzerland AG 2019
T. Cazenave et al. (Eds.): CGW 2018, CCIS 1017, pp. 127–146, 2019.
https://doi.org/10.1007/978-3-030-24337-1_7

to examine the obtained knowledge and the resulting programs, move prediction and playing strength are used as the most common evaluation methods. In this paper we investigate each of these methods and the impact of knowledge on the MCTS-based program Fuego.

In Sect. 2 first we briefly describe simple features. Then in Sect. 3 we introduce playing strength and move prediction as evaluation methods. We then describe the research motivations for this work in Sect. 4. Then in Sect. 5 we describe the experiments and analysis of the obtained result. In Sect. 6 we describe the conclusions and future work. This paper is a condensed version of the results in the first author's MSc thesis [12].

2   Knowledge and Simple Features

We define knowledge as information gained by training methods that helps a program to act in an informed manner, and improves the performance of a player when applied. One method of obtaining knowledge is by using features. Features are properties of a game state or a move, which can reveal information about that state or move. Examples of move features in Go are whether it captures any stone, or creates a ko situation. Coulom [6] defined a set of simple move features that were extensively used and extended by other programs. In order to use simple features, we need to evaluate them. Fuego uses Latent Factor Ranking (LFR) [16] as its evaluation and training method for simple features.

3   Evaluation Methods

3.1   Playing Strength

One method for testing knowledge is comparing playing strength with and without the use of that knowledge. In this scenario we use knowledge either as a standalone player or integrate it into an available program, and play a number of matches against other programs or another version of itself. If we know the level of strength of the opponent, then we can estimate the strength of our program from the obtained results by using the Elo rating formula [7]. If we integrate knowledge in an existing program, then we can estimate the quality of the knowledge by measuring the increase in playing strength resulting from the added knowledge.

3.2   Move Prediction

Move prediction is the act of predicting the next move in a game that was played before. To predict a move, we select a position from a game and feed that position to the game-playing engine. Then we compare the response received with the next move played in the game. Games played by professional players are one of the main data sources for training knowledge in Go. In order to evaluate the obtained knowledge move prediction is very often used.

Coulom [6] reported a 34.9% prediction rate for his feature-based knowledge learning technique. Wistuba et al. [16] were able to reach 40.9% prediction rate. Xiao et al. [20] were able to improve Wistuba's [16] method to increase the prediction rate by 2%. Clark et al. [5] used deep neural networks to increase the prediction rate to 44%. Soon after, Maddison et al. reached 55% with a deeper and larger network [15]. The current state of art in move predictors are deep residual networks [13]. Cazenave reports a 58% prediction rate with such an approach [4]. In general, stronger knowledge has led to stronger play. We want to measure whether in different Fuego-based players, increases in prediction rate correspond with increased playing strength.

4   Research Motivations

The relation between knowledge and search in Go programs and how these two impact each other is an area that still needs more study. Research motivations for this work are as following: 1. *Examine current evaluation approaches used in Go programs, which are: move prediction and playing against another program. Understand the differences between each of these tests and how they relate to each other*, 2. *Evaluate the impact of knowledge on the performance of a Go program*, 3. *How does longer and deeper search improve the strength of a MCTS program, in the presence of knowledge?*, and 4. *Can this increased strength be explained in terms of simple feature knowledge?*

Many researchers have studied simulation policies in Go, focusing on move prediction as an evaluation method, or comparing the strength of two programs [10,14,19]. Xiao et al. [21] report both improved move prediction and playing strength of Fuego after adding stronger knowledge; however, no insight is given to what those changes in the evaluation mean. Fernando et al. [9] analyze the Fuego simulation policy and the impact of changes to it. No analysis was done on evaluation methods and interpretation of the effect of added knowledge. Our current work is the first such analysis.

5   Experimental Results and Discussion

In this section we first we describe the players used in our experiments, then provide the results. We explain those results, and use them to investigate our research motivations.

5.1   Fuego-Based Players Used in Our Experiments

In our experiments we have used the following players from the Fuego code base.

Playout Policy-Only Player: this simple player uses only the playout policy of Fuego for generating the next move in the game, and it does not use search. This player helps us to understand the playout policy in Fuego better, and also helps us to measure different aspects of the playout policy, such as move prediction and playing strength.

Simple Features-Only Player: here, we use the prior knowledge in Fuego as a stand-alone player. The highest evaluated move according to features is played. Having a features-only player helps us to understand how the knowledge encoded in features compares to search, and it also helps to better evaluate feature knowledge.

No Knowledge Player: in order to examine how knowledge helps the performance of a player, we turn off prior knowledge and move filtering in Fuego. This player uses only MCTS with the default Fuego playout policy. This player helps us better understand the impact of search on a player's move prediction and playing strength.

No Additive Player: Fuego by default uses additive knowledge to help its in-tree policy focus more on high-ranking moves. We turn off the additive knowledge in this player, and rollback Fuego to use MCTS with the UCT method. This player helps us to better understand the role of additive knowledge in Fuego.

Default MCTS-Based Fuego Player: we need to be able to compare the results obtained by other players with full-strength Fuego. This player uses the full Fuego engine with all default settings.

Varying the Number of Simulations: for the MCTS-based players No Knowledge, No Additive and Default we vary the number of simulations in {100, 300, 1000, 3000, 10000}. This helps us to understand the impact of more search on different players.

5.2   Move Prediction

For the move prediction task, we used games from Pro Game Collection [3]. In total we used 4621 games, after removing games that were played on board sizes other than 19×19. Table 1 shows the results of the move prediction task on all the positions from these games. The players are Fuego-based engines described in Sect. 5.1. The move prediction rate is the fraction of positions for which the professional move was predicted correctly. For the No Knowledge, No Additive, and Default Fuego players the number in the name represents the number of simulations per move used by that player. Figure 1 shows the prediction rate for different number of simulations.

The Playout Policy-Only and Simple Features-Only players do not use Monte Carlo simulations. Playout Policy-Only predicted less than 22% of professional moves. Simple Features-Only has a much higher prediction rate of approximately 31%. Given the fact that neither of those two players uses MCTS, the gap signifies the role of the knowledge obtained through a large set of simple features trained by machine learning methods in the Simple Features-Only player, compared to the combination of fast rules and small patterns in the Playout Policy-Only player.

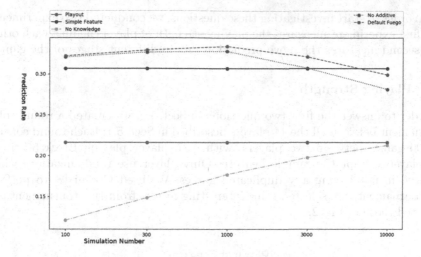

Fig. 1. Graph of move prediction rate.

Removing all knowledge has a big negative impact on the prediction rate in MCTS. It drops the prediction rate to 12% in the No Knowledge player with 100 simulations. Search compensates for the lack of knowledge to some degree. With 10000 simulations, the prediction rate of the No Knowledge player increases to over 21%. Nonetheless, this is still far below the move prediction rate of any MCTS player utilizing knowledge. This shows the role of knowledge in giving direction to MCTS toward nodes with better outlook, when the number of simulations is limited.

The prediction rate of the No Additive player is between approximately 28% and 33%. Up to 1000 simulations, increasing the number of simulations improves the prediction rate; however, after that it starts to drop. When we compare the results of a No Additive player to the Default MCTS-based player with the same number of simulations, we observe a similar pattern in change of prediction rate. The difference between prediction rates of the Default Fuego player and the No Additive player for simulations between 100 to 10000 are: 0.0015, 0.0024, 0.0061, 0.0139, 0.0178. This shows that as the number of simulations grows, additive knowledge slows down the drop of prediction rate in the Default Fuego player, and biases the selection policy in MCTS more towards professional player moves. This widening gap can also be observed in Fig. 1.

Given the obtained results several new questions arise:

- Is there any difference in strength between players with similar prediction rate?
- What role does the number of simulations play in players strength vs prediction rate?
- Why does the prediction rate for No Additive and Default MCTS players start to drop?

In order to start investigating these questions, we conducted two experiments. The first experiment measures the playing strength of players against each other. The second measures the move prediction rate in different stages of the games.

5.3   Playing Strength

In order to answer the first two questions in Sect. 5.2, we created a round robin tournament between all the 11 players described in Sect. 5.1. Each round consists of 100 games between two players, with each player playing Black 50 times. All players except the Simple Features-Only player use randomization, which resulted in not having any duplicated games. We used GoGui [2] to perform the tournament. We selected some interesting results from this tournament and reported those in Fig. 2.

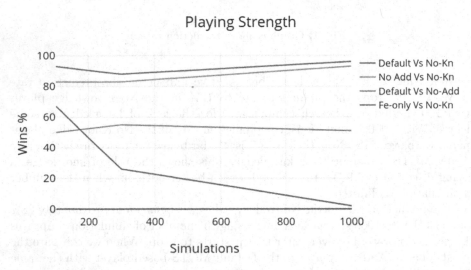

Fig. 2. Result of 100 game matches between pairs of players.

Default MCTS-Based Fuego vs No Additive Player. This compares the experiments with same number of simulations between the No Additive and default MCTS-based Fuego player. Increasing simulations does not change the balance of strength between these two settings, and removing additive knowledge had minimal impact on playing strength. This is consistent with what we observed in the move prediction task. It can be concluded from the result that these two players have almost the same playing strength against each other when using the same number of simulations.

No Knowledge vs Other MCTS-Based Players. The playing strength of the No Knowledge player decreases most of the time against an opponent with the same number of simulations as the number of simulations increases. The role of knowledge becomes more important as a player's strength increases. Knowledge helps a player to avoid crucial mistakes in a game, where a stronger opponent can better exploit those mistakes. While it seems that more search should compensate for lack of knowledge, there are two reasons that we do not see that effect in this group of experiments. First, the opponent also benefits from an increased number of simulations. Second, in a player that uses the knowledge, increasing the number of simulations leads to more visits of promising moves that the knowledge picks. This enables the player to examine these moves more deeply, and pick the best among them. The No Knowledge player is less focused and needs more simulations to achieve the same effect.

Varying Number of Simulations, 300 vs 100. As expected from previous experience with MCTS-based engines, we can see that in every case, a 3x increase in number of simulations leads to a huge difference in playing strength. This is in sharp contrast to the move prediction task in Table 1, where the difference was small and sometimes even negative. This shows that using the move prediction rate as a measure to examine a player is not as informative as we expected it to be. There remain aspects of a player which strongly affect its comparative strength against another player, which move prediction is unable to reveal.

No Additive vs Other MCTS-Based Players. In these experiments, removing the additive term has limited impact on playing strength. The biggest change in playing strength between the No Additive and Default Fuego player is in 300 simulations, where Default Fuego player won 55% of games. Removing feature knowledge decreases the playing strength by a huge margin, with win-rates of only 7–17% for the No Knowledge player.

Simple Features-Only vs No Knowledge Players. This scaling experiment shows how much search is needed to reach and surpass Simple Feature knowledge. With 100 simulations, the No Knowledge player is weaker than feature knowledge: it loses 67 games. With 300 simulations, the No knowledge player surpasses the strength of the Simple Features-Only player, and with 1000 simulations the No Knowledge player is much stronger, winning 98 of 100 games.

5.4   A Closer Look at Move Prediction Rate

In Sect. 5.2 of the previous experiment, surprisingly the move prediction rate did not show any major difference between Default Fuego and the No additive player when the number of simulations was varied between 100 to 1000, while Sect. 5.3 showed undeniable differences in strength between those players. We also want to understand why the prediction rate starts to drop after 3000 simulations in the

Default MCTS-based and No Additive players. In this experiment, we study the effect of the game phase. We divide a game into six intervals from the opening to the endgame, and measure the prediction accuracy of each player separately for each interval. We created six intervals of 50 moves each, corresponding to move 0 to move 300. Because of the limited number of available samples after move 300 we ignored those final small endgame moves.

Figure 3 shows the move prediction accuracy per interval for Default Fuego with 100 and 1000 simulations, and for No Additive with 100 and 1000 simulations. While Table 1 showed no noticeable difference between 100 and 1000 simulations, Fig. 3 shows that for the first 200 moves there is a major difference in both Default Fuego and No Additive players, with a higher prediction rate for the 1000 simulation player. This difference fades from moves 200–250 and turns to the opposite for moves 251–300.

Figure 4 shows the prediction accuracy for experiments where we saw the drop of prediction rate with 3000 and 10000 simulations for No Additive and Default Fuego. We added the 300 simulation players as a baseline. In the opening, the prediction rate for the Default Fuego players increases with number of simulations, and for No Additive players remains very similar for the first 50 moves. From the second interval to the last, the prediction rate of the 300 simulation players sharply increases. For the 3000 simulation players this increase is more moderate. In the 10000 simulation players we observe a drop of prediction rates for the first 250 moves, and then a slight rebound.

To explain the lower prediction rate in the late endgame in players using more simulations, we need to look at how the selection policy in MCTS works. In a game when one player's winning probability is very high, there are many moves that still result in that player winning, while being sub-optimal in terms of score. The selection policy in Fuego maximizes winning probability, not score. After 200 moves, the winner of most of the games can be predicted with high confidence. Fuego chooses a "safest" move according to its noisy simulations. Professional players will not usually select such point-losing "safe" moves. Another reason lies in the impact of knowledge on players with fewer simulations. Knowledge is used to initialize the value of a node in the Monte Carlo tree. When the number of simulations is still small, this initialization plays a major role in MCTS search. Since it is based on features learned from professional games, it biases the search toward professional moves. As the number of simulations grows, its impact diminishes.

5.5   Move Prediction and Feature Frequency

Since the move prediction rate alone does not explain the difference in playing strength, we try to find other differentiating factors between various players by focusing on features. Features play a major role in the success of a player. Even modern neural networks can be seen as a function that is built upon a complex set of features computed in its nodes. In order to understand the significance of different features, we use frequency of features, and we report the most frequent features for each experiment. We count the number of times each feature

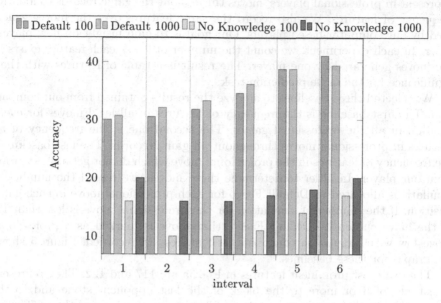

Fig. 3. Move prediction accuracy per game phase for 100 and 1000 simulation players. Each group has 50 moves.

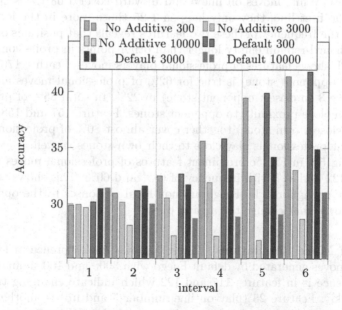

Fig. 4. Move prediction accuracy per game phase for 300, 3000 ad 10000 simulation players. Each group has 50 moves.

is present in professional players' moves throughout the game records to identify frequency of features. We also record the same features over the moves generated by our computer-based players. Our goal is to gain insight on how players differ. In each experiment, we count the number of times each feature exists in the moves generated by one player. The result is a table of features with their significance for the move prediction task.

We selected three baselines to analyze the results obtained from our comparison. The first baseline is the frequency of features in all legal moves for every position in all the professional games. The second one is the frequency of all features in professional moves throughout all game records. The last baseline is the frequency of features in the professional move which do not get any attention from our player. In order to determine these moves, we record the number of simulations allocated by Default Fuego for each professional move in each game position. If the number of simulation for the professional move is less than 1% of the move chosen by Default Fuego, that move is marked as a professional move low with simulation count and its features are recorded. Figure 5 shows the graphs for these baselines.

The two most prominent features in Fig. 5a are 117 and 122. They represent a distance of 4 or more to the block of the last opponent stone and to the block of the last own stone respectively. Their frequency is more than 85% over all legal moves for each position. This is not surprising due to the size of the 19×19 board, and the distribution of legal moves in each position. The next two prominent features are 25 (moves on line 5 and upward) and 21 (moves on the first line). While moves on line 5 and upward cover 1.68 times the area of moves on the first line, they only happen 1.25 times more in the legal moves. Comparing the frequency of these two features reveals that positions on the first line of the board remain empty longer than other points in professional games.

Figure 5b shows features of professional players moves. Feature 176 (distance 2 to closest opponent stone) is true for 62% of professional moves and feature 177 (distance 3 to closest opponent stone) in 22%. In total 85% of professional moves are in close proximity to opponent stones. Feature 157 and 158 (distance 2 and 3 to closest own stone) together cover almost 80% of professional moves, showing that professionals play close to their own stones as well.

As in Fig. 5a, in Fig. 5c prominent features of professional moves missed by Fuego are 122 and 117 with frequency of 68% and 60%. This shows that moves that usually get ignored by Fuego are non-local responses to the opponent, or "tenuki" moves that change the area of play.

Impact of More Simulations. Figure 6 shows the difference in feature frequency of moves generated by default Fuego with 3000 and 100 simulations. The main difference is in features 117 and 122 which indicate changing the area of play, "tenuki". Feature 25 (play on line number 5 and up) is another example of the impact of more simulations on the area of play. We saw that this is one of the prominent features of professional players moves. These results show that

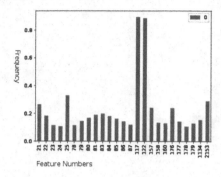

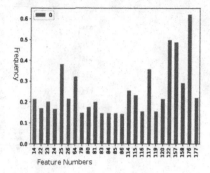

(a) Feature frequencies of every legal move in professional games.

(b) Feature frequencies of all professional moves in professional games.

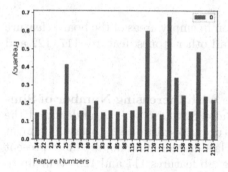

(c) Features of professional moves that have low number of simulations compared to the move played by Default Fuego using 1000 simulations.

Fig. 5. Feature counts of baselines.

the player with more simulations can find centre and tenuki moves more often, and becomes more similar to how professional players play in these situations.

Impact of the Additive Term. Figures 7a and b show the differences between the default Fuego player and the No additive player with 3000 simulations. In Fig. 7a, features 157 and 176 are for playing in distance of 2 to the closest own stone and opponent colour respectively. They happen 6% and 4% more in the default Fuego player which benefits from the additive term. This shows that additive knowledge encourages playing close to previous stones. Feature 64 also happens 3% more in the player using the additive term. This feature is for 3×3 patterns used in the simulations policy. This is an expected behaviour as the additive knowledge uses a local shape pattern to evaluate each move. Other features in Fig. 7a have a very low frequency.

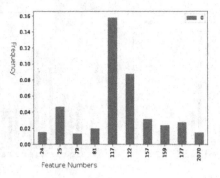

Fig. 6. Top 10 differences between features count of default Fuego player with 3000 simulations and 100 simulations.

The No Additive player plays more often in empty areas of the board (feature 2153, 3×3 empty pattern), and far from all other stones, features 117, 122 and 160 (distance 5 to closest own stone).

Impact of Simple Feature Knowledge with Increasing Number of Simulations. By comparing Figs. 8a and b and 8c and d we can understand the impact of simple feature knowledge. Features 26 (distance 2 to last opponent stone), 64 and 114 (distance 1 to block of last opponent stone) are more present in the player with knowledge, while in Fig. 8b features 117 and 122 occur up to 42% more in the No Knowledge player. This shows that the No Knowledge player with low number of simulations plays more randomly in all areas of the board without any attention to the last own or opponent move, while the player with knowledge responds locally to those moves more often.

As the number of simulations grows, we still observe in Figs. 8c and d the same difference in style of play from default Fuego and the No Knowledge player. This gap, however, narrows to half with consistency in relative frequency of features to each other. To some degree more simulations compensate for the lack of knowledge in the No Knowledge player, as we already observed in the move prediction task; however, more simulations are not able to completely close the gap.

Features of Professional Moves. We ran another experiment to understand why some professional moves are ignored in Fuego. We compared the statistics of the default Fuego moves to the professional moves with low simulations in Fig. 9. This helps to understand what kind of moves professional players make that Fuego does not consider, and how often those moves happen. In Fig. 9a, features 114, 115, 119, 157, 176 are all for moves with distance of 1 or 2 to the own or opponent stones. This signifies the higher degree of locality of play in Fuego versus professional players. Also 3×3 simulation policy patterns (feature 64) occur 35% more in the default Fuego moves than in professional moves with low number of simulations, showing that many professional moves do not follow

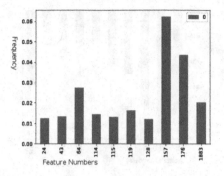

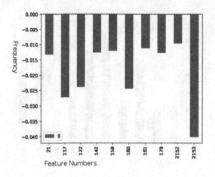

(a) Top 10 positive differences.   (b) Top 10 negative differences.

Fig. 7. Difference between feature counts of default Fuego and No Additive player when both players use 3000 simulations.

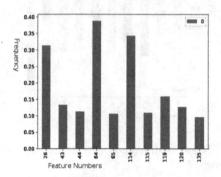

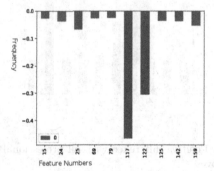

(a) Top 10 positive difference when both players use 100 simulations.

(b) Bottom 10 negative difference when both players use 100 simulations.

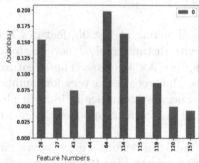

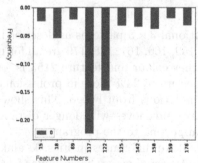

(c) Top 10 positive difference when both players use 3000 simulations.

(d) Bottom 10 negative difference when both players use 3000 simulations.

Fig. 8. Difference between feature counts of default Fuego and No Knowledge player.

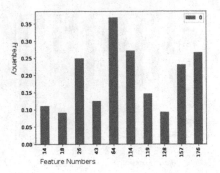 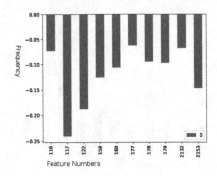

(a) Positive difference with professional moves low simulation count.

(b) Negative difference with professional moves with low simulation count.

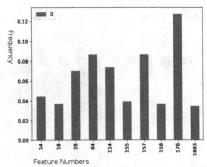 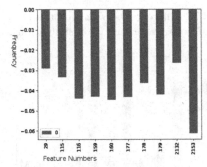

(c) Positive difference with all professional moves.

(d) Negative difference with all professional moves.

Fig. 9. Difference between feature counts of default Fuego with 3000 simulations moves and professional moves.

traditional 3×3 patterns as described in [11]. Looking at Fig. 9b, features 117, 122, 159, 160, 161, 178, 179 are all for moves with distance of 4 or more to stones of either colour and feature 2153 is for the empty 3×3 square. These features happen up to 24% more in professional moves that received a very low number of simulations from Fuego. This shows that Fuego systematically likes to play locally, and moves with longer distance to the last own or opponent stone are not appealing to the program.

Feature differences in Figs. 9c and d between the default Fuego moves and all professional moves have similar feature differences to Figs. 9a and b, but with different magnitude. First the magnitude of difference is much lower in Figs. 9c and d. The other difference is that the most differentiating factor for the default Fuego player is that it plays 12% more in distance 2 of opponent stones (feature 176) than professional players. Professional moves still occur more in distance of 3 or more (features 116, 159, 160, 177, 178 and 179) to other stones, but the gap to Fuego is smaller.

5.6   Move Selection Analysis

The next experiment helps us to understand under what circumstances a player can predict a professional move, while at other times it can not. We created an experiment to measure the number of simulations relative to the initial weight of a move. The results of this experiment are reported in Fig. 10.

For the Y-axis of Fig. 10 we measured two different cases. In the first case, we measured the number of simulations $sim_{s,a}$ for move a in state s relative to the total number of simulations for state s in the professional game: $\frac{sim_{s,a}}{\Sigma_i sim_{s,i}}$. For the second case, we measured the relative number of simulations $sim_{s,a}$ for move a in state s to the number of simulation $sim_{s,b}$ for move b in state s: $\frac{sim_{s,a}}{sim_{s,b}}$. The Y-axis of Figs. 10a to d use the first case. For Figs. 10a and b, move a is the move selected by default Fuego, and for Figs. 10c and d it is the move selected by the professional player. The Y-axis of Figs. 10e and f uses the second case. Move a is the move selected by the professional player and move b is the move selected by default Fuego.

The X-axis of Fig. 10 has two different formats. In the first one, we use the initial weight $w_{s,a}$ of move a in state s of the professional game. For the second case, we compute the maximum weight $w_{s,max}$ for the state s, then compute the relative weight of move a to the maximum weight $\frac{w_{s,a}}{w_{s,max}}$. Since the weight of a move can be negative, we normalize the relative value by a sigmoid function $\frac{sig(w_a)}{sig(w_{max})}$. The X-axis of Figs. 10a, c and e uses the first format. The X-axis of Figs. 10b, d and f uses the second format. Move a is selected by default Fuego in Figs. 10a and b, and by professional players in Figs. 10c and f.

In order to understand the distribution of simulations, we created Fig. 11a. It represents the relation between the weight of the feature for a move selected by default Fuego and the percent of simulations that move has received. Most of the moves selected by default Fuego have the majority of the simulations. Moves with higher initial weights receive almost 100% of simulations. Moves selected by Fuego have different ranges of weights from low to high. However, Fig. 10b shows that even moves with low weights have weights close to the maximum weight of that position, and most of the times are the maximum weight.

Figure 10c shows that professional players moves most of the time either received the maximum number of simulations, or received close to zero. Moves that have an in-between number of simulations make up a smaller portion of professional moves. Figure 10d better illustrates this point. Figure 11b shows that for professional moves to get the attention of Fuego, they need to have higher evaluation by simple features.

We also compared the number of simulations for the professional moves and the moves selected by default Fuego. Figure 10e shows that very often the move played by professionals is the same as the Fuego move. However, if they differ, the chances of the professional move having a large number of simulations is low. Most of the time, it has less than 20% compared to Fuego's move. Figure 10f plots the relative number of simulations and the relative heuristic weight of the professional move to the move selected by default Fuego. The ratio of simulations

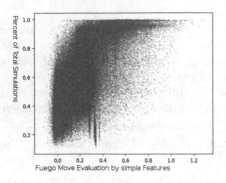

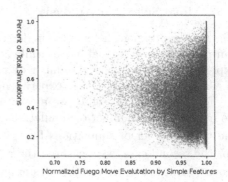

(a) Graph of selected move by default Fuego player given its initial weight

(b) Graph of selected move by default Fuego player given sigmoid of its initial weight divided by sigmoid of Max weight.

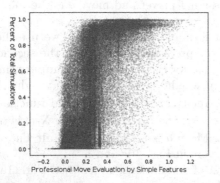

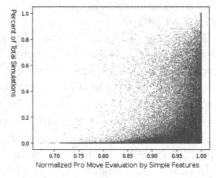

(c) Graph of played move by professional player given its initial weight.

(d) Graph of selected move by professional Player given its sigmoid of its initial weight divided by sigmoid of Max weight.

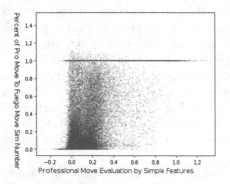

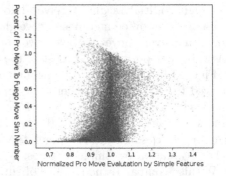

(e) Percent of simulations relative to selected move divided by professional player's move given its initial weight.

(f) Percent of simulations relative to selected move divided by professional player's move given sigmoid of its initial weight divided by sigmoid of Max weight.

Fig. 10. Comparison between number of simulations for initial feature weight.

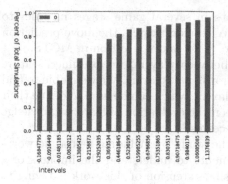 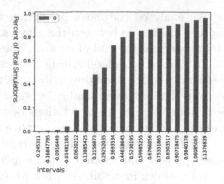

(a) Graph of average simulations for se-lected move by default Fuego player given its initial weight.

(b) Graph of average simulations for selected move by default professional player given its initial weight.

Fig. 11. Percent of average number of simulations for buckets of initial weights.

drops sharply as the relative weight of the professional player's move decreases. For professional moves that have a ratio of less than 0.9, their number of simulations is near zero most of the time. Less than 7% of professional moves have both higher weight than the move selected by Fuego, and fewer simulations.

This experiment showed us the importance of simple feature initialization on the number of simulations a move receives. Fuego gives professional moves more simulations if they have high evaluation by simple features and ignores them if their simple feature evaluation is low.

The move selected by Fuego does not need to have high evaluation as seen in Fig. 10a. It just needs to have an evaluation close to the maximum move evaluation of that position. This can be observed in Fig. 10b. We also observed in Figs. 10d and e how professional moves either receive close to the maximum number of simulations or close to zero.

6   Conclusions and Future Work

In this work we investigated two popular evaluation methods: move prediction and playing strength, and how they relate to each other. We noticed that move prediction did not reveal important aspects of a player, and there remain many details that an aggregated move prediction percentage can not express. Players with similar move prediction rate can have very different playing strengths.

We used a playing strength experiment to understand the impact of the following concepts in MCTS: additive knowledge, simple feature knowledge, number of simulations, and playout policy. The additive term has a very small impact on playing strength. Removing feature knowledge has a massive negative impact on playing strength which only increases with more search.

We analyzed the move prediction rate in several game stages in order to capture differences between the players. With more search, the move prediction rate drops near the end of a game, due to "safe" move selection in MCTS.

To find more differentiating factors between players, we examined feature frequencies in the move prediction task for different players. We were able to find features that differ remarkably between players, which can be used to define their behaviour. We also found relations between the evaluation of feature knowledge and the number of simulations a move receives.

For future work, we want to extend the study by including neural network-based players and extending the experiments to understand the impacts of a neural network in detail. Another promising extension of this work is trying to understand neural networks in terms of both simple features and move prediction, in order to find an interpretation of their behaviour with known features of the Go game.

Acknowledgement. Financial support was provided by NSERC, The Natural Sciences and Engineering Research Council of Canada.

A   Detailed Move Prediction Results

Table 1. Result of move prediction for players based on Fuego.

Experiment	Accuracy
Playout policy-only	0.2160
Simple features-only	0.3066
No knowledge 100	0.1212
No knowledge 300	0.1486
No knowledge 1000	0.1767
No knowledge 3000	0.1976
No knowledge 10000	0.2125
No additive 100	0.3209
No additive 300	0.3269
No additive 1000	0.3281
No additive 3000	0.3074
No additive 10000	0.2811
Default 100	0.3224
Default 300	0.3293
Default 1000	0.3342
Default 3000	0.3213
Default 10000	0.2989

References

1. Fuego Source Code. http://fuego.sourceforge.net, SVN revision 2032. Accessed 16 Aug 2016
2. GoGui Project. https://sourceforge.net/projects/gogui/. Accessed 14 Dec 2016
3. Professional Games. https://badukmovies.com/pro_games. Accessed 02 Nov 2016
4. Cazenave, T.: Residual networks for computer Go. IEEE Trans. Games **10**(1), 107–110 (2018)
5. Clark, C., Storkey, A.: Training deep convolutional neural networks to play Go. In: International Conference on Machine Learning, pp. 1766–1774 (2015)
6. Coulom, R.: Computing Elo ratings of move patterns in the game of Go. In: van den Herik, H.J., Winands, M., Uiterwijk, J., Schadd, M. (eds.) Computer Games Workshop, Amsterdam, Netherlands, June 2007
7. Elo, A.E.: The Rating of Chessplayers, Past and Present. Arco Publishing, New York (1978)
8. Enzenberger, M., Müller, M., Arneson, B., Segal, R.: Fuego an open-source framework for board games and Go engine based on Monte Carlo tree search. IEEE Trans. Comput. Intell. AI Games **2**(4), 259–270 (2010)
9. Fernando, S., Müller, M.: Analyzing simulations in Monte Carlo tree search for the game of Go. In: Computers and Games - 8th International Conference, CG 2013, Yokohama, Japan, 13–15 August 2013, Revised Selected Papers, pp. 72–83 (2013)
10. Gelly, S., Silver, D.: Combining online and offline knowledge in UCT. In: Proceedings of the 24th International Conference on Machine Learning, pp. 273–280. ACM (2007)
11. Gelly, S., Wang, Y., Munos, R., Teytaud, O.: Modification of UCT with patterns in Monte Carlo Go (2006)
12. Haqiqat, F.: Analyzing the impact of knowledge and search in Monte Carlo tree search in Go. Master's thesis, University of Alberta (2018)
13. He, K., Zhang, X., Ren, S., Sun, J.: Deep residual learning for image recognition. In: Proceedings of the IEEE Conference on Computer Vision and Pattern Recognition, pp. 770–778 (2016)
14. Huang, S.-C., Coulom, R., Lin, S.-S.: Monte-Carlo simulation balancing in practice. In: van den Herik, H.J., Iida, H., Plaat, A. (eds.) CG 2010. LNCS, vol. 6515, pp. 81–92. Springer, Heidelberg (2011). https://doi.org/10.1007/978-3-642-17928-0_8
15. Maddison, C.J., Huang, A., Sutskever, I., Silver, D.: Move evaluation in Go using deep convolutional neural networks. International Conference on Learning Representations. arXiv preprint arXiv:1412.6564 (2014)
16. Wistuba, M., Schmidt-Thieme, L.: Move prediction in Go – modelling feature interactions using latent factors. In: Timm, I.J., Thimm, M. (eds.) KI 2013. LNCS (LNAI), vol. 8077, pp. 260–271. Springer, Heidelberg (2013). https://doi.org/10.1007/978-3-642-40942-4_23
17. Silver, D., et al.: Mastering the game of Go with deep neural networks and tree search. Nature **529**(7587), 484–489 (2016)
18. Silver, D., et al.: Mastering the game of Go without human knowledge. Nature **550**(7676), 354–359 (2017)
19. Silver, D., Tesauro, G.: Monte Carlo simulation balancing. In: Proceedings of the 26th Annual International Conference on Machine Learning, ICML 2009, pp. 945–952. ACM, New York (2009)

20. Xiao, C., Müller, M.: Factorization ranking model for move prediction in the game of Go. In: AAAI, pp. 1359–1365 (2016)
21. Xiao, C., Müller, M.: Integrating factorization ranked features in MCTS: an experimental study. In: Cazenave, T., Winands, M.H.M., Edelkamp, S., Schiffel, S., Thielscher, M., Togelius, J. (eds.) CGW/GIGA -2016. CCIS, vol. 705, pp. 34–43. Springer, Cham (2017). https://doi.org/10.1007/978-3-319-57969-6_3

What's in a Game? The Effect of Game Complexity on Deep Reinforcement Learning

Erdem Emekligil$^{(\boxtimes)}$ and Ethem Alpaydın

Department of Computer Engineering, Boğaziçi University, 34342 Istanbul, Turkey
{erdem.emekligil,alpaydin}@boun.edu.tr

Abstract. Deep Reinforcement Learning (DRL) combines deep neural networks with reinforcement learning. These methods, unlike their predecessors, learn end-to-end by extracting high-dimensional representations from raw sensory data to directly predict the actions. DRL methods were shown to master most of the ATARI games, beating humans in a good number of them, using the same algorithm, network architecture and hyper-parameters. However, why DRL works on some games better than others has not been fully investigated. In this paper, we propose that the complexity of each game is defined by a number of factors (the size of the search space, existence/absence of enemies, existence/absence of intermediate reward, and so on) and we posit that how fast and well a game is learned by DRL depends on these factors. Towards this aim, we use simplified Maze and Pacman environments and we conduct experiments to see the effect of such factors on the convergence of DRL. Our results provide a first step in a better understanding of how DRL works and as such will be informative in the future in determining scenarios where DRL can be applied effectively e.g., outside of games.

Keywords: Deep reinforcement learning · Computer games

1 Introduction

In their seminal work, Mnih et al. [10] show that a Deep Q-learning Network (DQN) can learn to play ATARI 2600 games end-to-end. The neural network takes the raw screen image as input, which it processes through a number of layers (first convolutional, then fully-connected), and its output units directly control the actions of the joystick. They show that DQN needs no fine-tuning for each task and that using the same learning algorithm, network architecture and hyper-parameters, any one of the 49 games can be learned.

They report that DQN "outperforms competing methods in almost all the games, and performs at a level that is broadly compatible with or superior to a professional human games tester in the majority of games." They also note that "the games in which DQN excels are extremely varied in their nature," but that

© Springer Nature Switzerland AG 2019
T. Cazenave et al. (Eds.): CGW 2018, CCIS 1017, pp. 147–163, 2019.
https://doi.org/10.1007/978-3-030-24337-1_8

"games demanding more temporally extended planning strategies still constitute a major challenge."

Our main idea in this paper is that there are factors that define the complexity of a game and that games that may appear different at first glance may actually be similar in terms of such abstract factors, or vice versa. For instance, whether the player is the only agent or if there are other agents, possibly hostile, that can act is such a factor. We assume not only that there are such factors but also that the speed a game is learned, e.g., by DQN, depends on these factors.

In this work, we are going to take the DQN as it is and test it on a number of settings where we vary such factors. It should be noted here that our aim is *not* to understand how DQN learns a particular task (game) or what its hidden units or layers are doing to handle that task, but rather we take the totality of DQN (the network, learning algorithm, and hyper-parameters) as a black-box and want to see what type of task attributes affect DQN's performance and how. The settings we use is simple by design so that we can easily observe the effect of changes on DQN's convergence. We believe that such a study is informative in understanding where and how DQN, or similar approaches, can best be used, and finding out such abstract factors that define a learning task and how such factors effect learning will especially be useful when we want to use models like DQN outside of the game-playing domain.

2   Background

The DQN takes four consecutive screen images as input which it processes by three convolutional and then two fully-connected layers with a final output layer where there is one output for each valid joystick action. Q-learning is used to update the network weights, with experience replay to randomize over data. We do not discuss DQN any further here; the interested reader is referred to [10].

Since then, the related literature can be divided into two, as work where DQN is generalized for other tasks, and works that strive to improve the performance of DQN.

As examples of the first, Levine et al. [7] use supervised learning before reinforcement learning for more complex tasks. Similarly in AlphaGo, Silver et al. [14] take advantage of supervised data to initially train a network that evaluates the Go board. They combine Monte Carlo tree search with a DQN variant to create an agent that is able to beat the human player with the second best Elo rating at the time. AlphaGo Zero [16] goes one step further and is trained without any supervised data, and is able to beat AlphaGo. Alpha Zero [15], which is the generalized version of AlphaGo Zero, learns to play Shogi and Chess better than the best computer programs for each game. DQN is also used outside of the domain of game-playing; for example, a version with 1D convolution is used for simulating animal movements [12]. It is also altered for control tasks such as cart-pole, locomotion and car driving problems by using deep function approximators [8].

As improvements to DQN, Double-DQN (DDQN) uses a backup network as the target action value function [5]. The actual network is used for selecting the action with the maximum value whereas the target network is used for estimating that action's value. Instead of random picks in experience replay, Schaul et al. [13] define different methods to prioritize the picks from replay memory and show that prioritizing achieve major improvements. Wang et al. [17] introduce a new architecture that combines a state value function and an action advantage function. DQN is also adapted to work on distributed [11] and multi-core CPU systems [9] using actor-critic (A3C) methods with LSTMs. Unlike previous methods, Distributional DQN [2] can distinguish risky actions and the Rainbow method [6] unites six previous developments over DQN and show that these different methods achieve better results when they are combined.

3 Factors that Define a Game

It is our contention in this paper that games that seem very different at first glance may be very similar at a more abstract level and beyond their immediate facade, games can be defined in terms of a number of factors, and furthermore it is these factors that define the complexity of a game and the best strategy to play it well.

There is previous work on the various characteristics of games and how they effect playability, by humans and AI programs; see the book by Elias et al. [4]. Anderson et al. [1] compare performances of several tree-based search algorithms such as MinMax, MCTS and A* on seven different games that they have created. Yannakakis et al. [18] define five different factors based on [4] and explain their effects on AI methods:

- Number of players. Is the game played by a single player or multiple players, or does a single player play with/against computer controlled enemy units?
- Stochasticity. Does the outcome of the game determined only by the player?
- Time granularity. Is the game turn-based or real-time?
- Observability. Is the game partially observable or the player has perfect information?
- Action space size. The number of the actions the player can take.

In our case, we take DQN as the game-learner and consider games that can be learned by DQN, similar to the ATARI 2600 games, where we can define and test the effect of such factors.

We start by clustering the ATARI 2600 games according to how DQN learns them. We run DQN on 45 games and for each we record the convergence of DQN in terms average game scores. We then use dynamic time-warping (DTW) [3] to measure the distance between vectors of different lengths, each normalized between 0 and 1, since each game runs for a different number of epochs. The dendrogram achieved using average-linkage hierarchical clustering is shwown in Fig. 1, with convergence plots of some example games.

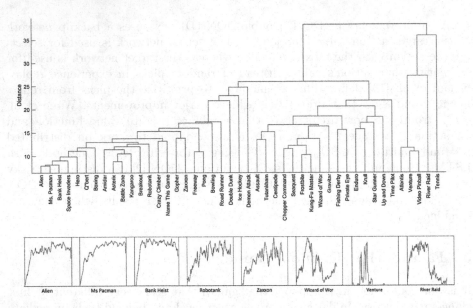

Fig. 1. Hierarchical clustering results of ATARI games, and the convergence of DQN on some example games.

Games whose convergence plots are similar are placed nearby in the tree and for certain cases, we can see that actually they correlate with similarities between the games.

For example, Ms Pacman and Alien, connected early on, are very similar both in terms of how DQN learns them and also in terms of how they are played. They are similar in many aspects such as actions, objective, rewards and so on; in both games, the agent tries to collect as many reward (food items) as possible without getting caught by the enemy and both have power-up units that temporarily give the ability to destroy opponents. Interestingly, Bank Heist looks similar to these but in Bank Heist, instead of power-up, the agent can counter enemies by bombs which changes the strategy. This difference changes the convergence of DQN and this explains the distance of Bank Heist to Ms Pacman and Alien on the tree.

Wizard of Wor and Alien are games that look very similar visually, but they are played differently and hence the convergence behavior of DQN is different and they are very distant in the dendrogram despite their visual similarity. River Raid and Venture are two games on which DQN fails and that is why they are on the same cluster. In Zaxxon and Robotank, the agent controls an airplane, a tank and the main objective is survival whether from an airplane or a tank crash. The games look similar, are played similarly and DQN convergence curves on them are similar and that is why they are not far from each other on the dendrogram.

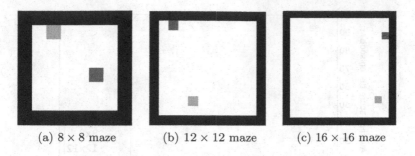

(a) 8 × 8 maze   (b) 12 × 12 maze   (c) 16 × 16 maze

Fig. 2. Example mazes of different sizes with outer walls (black), the target (dark gray) and the agent (light gray).

4   Maze Experiments

In this simple Maze task, the objective of the agent is to get to the stationary target by moving one square, horizontally or vertically, in each step. The position of the agent and the target are randomly chosen in each episode and a score of 100 is awarded when the agent reaches the target before the maximum number of allowed moves ((Width + Height) * 10).

In our experiments, we keep the original DQN network, learning algorithm, and hyper-parameters of [10][1] and test it first on a maze. The only parameter changed is the decay rate ϵ, which is adapted to the complexity of the maze by setting it to its minimal value that allows convergence. Since our generated mazes are much smaller, they are stretched to fit 84 × 84; the mazes contain the outer walls so the actual playable area is one less on all four sides. Each agent is evaluated after every 250,000 training frames for 125,000 test frames and the average episode score is plotted.

4.1   The Effect of the Size of the Search Space

We start by testing the effect of the maze size, which is an indication of the search space: A larger maze requires longer sequences of actions. We use mazes of 8 × 8, 12 × 12 and 16 × 16. A maze contains only the outer walls, the agent and the target. The walls are colored white, the target is dark gray, the agent is light gray. The background is black (encoded as 0) to help the network to learn faster (see Fig. 2; the colors are inverted to save from ink). We did five runs with different random seeds and plot the one that best represents the average behavior.

Because increasing the maze size increases the average number of actions required to get to the goal, as expected, and as we see in Fig. 3, the number of training epochs it takes for DQN to converge also increases.

---

[1] We expand and use Nathan Sprague's replication: https://github.com/spragunr/deep_q_rl.

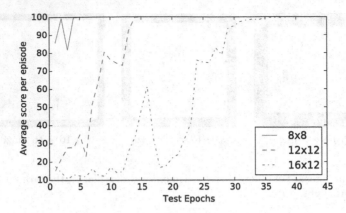

Fig. 3. Convergence of DQN as a function of maze size. As expected, larger mazes take longer to learn.

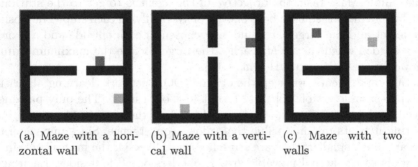

(a) Maze with a hori-   (b) Maze with a verti-   (c) Maze with two
zontal wall   cal wall   walls

Fig. 4. Example 12 × 12 mazes.

4.2   The Effect of Obstacles

The complexity of the path to solve the maze can be increased by adding obstacles. The agent cannot just take any path to the goal but needs to recognize and avoid the obstacles. In our experiments, we simulate this by a wall with a single gate. The positions of agent and target, as well as the location of the gate and the wall orientation are also randomly assigned in each episode. To make the task more complex, we also experimented with two intersecting walls that divide the maze into four playable areas connected by three randomly located gates. Randomly generated examples are shown in Fig. 4.

We trained DQN on these three setups with different obstacle structures (no wall, one wall, two walls) and three different sizes just like in the previous experiment. In Fig. 5, we see that because adding walls increases the path complexity and consequently the number of actions to achieve the goal, convergence of DQN is much slower needing more training iterations; with larger mazes, the differences get larger.

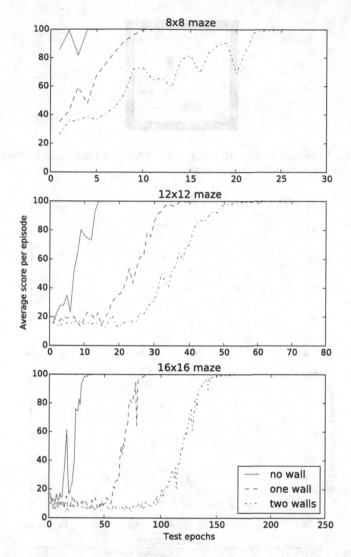

Fig. 5. Convergence of DQN as a function of maze sizes and wall structures. With more obstacles, learning gets slower.

4.3   The Effect of Hostile Agents

If the game-player is not the only agent that can change the environment, the presence and actions of other agents make the task harder. In our maze experiments, we added stationary unit-sized enemies that ends the game on contact (without any reward), to test if the network can learn to recognize and avoid them efficiently. As shown in Fig. 6, a different gray level is chosen to encode

Fig. 6. A 12×12 sample maze with outer walls (black), a target (dark gray), an agent (light gray) and four enemies (medium gray).

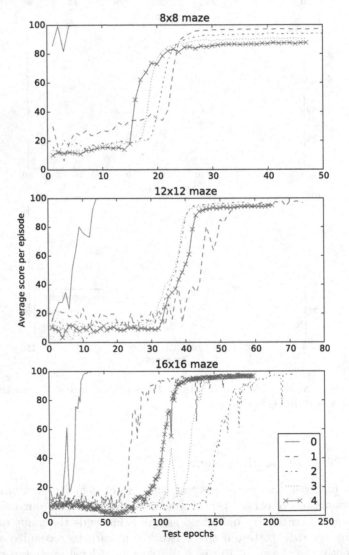

Fig. 7. Convergence of DQN as a function of maze size and the number of enemies. It is whether there is any enemy or not, rather than the number of enemies, that slows down learning.

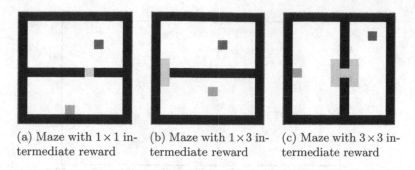

(a) Maze with 1×1 intermediate reward   (b) Maze with 1×3 intermediate reward   (c) Maze with 3×3 intermediate reward

Fig. 8. 12×12 mazes with different sizes of intermediate rewards.

the enemy, and the locations of these enemy units are chosen randomly in each episode.

Our results are given in Fig. 7, where we see that the presence of an enemy makes the task harder to learn, regardless of maze size. The number of enemies, as long as it is nonzero, does not seem to have a drastic effect. Plots with 2, 3, 4 enemies seem to be clustered together for mazes of 8×8 and 12×12; for the maze of 16×16, we believe that the variability is due to chance. Once DQN learns to recognize an enemy and how to avoid it, and it is enough to do enough episodes with a single enemy for that, DQN can then recognize and avoid any number of enemies that it later encounters.

4.4 The Effect of Intermediate Reward

In most games, the reward is given not only at the end but also at some special intermediate state, such as destroying an enemy unit or passing through a checkpoint. Such an intermediate reward is useful in hinting the learning agent that it is on the correct path to the goal. In our maze experiments, we implement this in the case with one wall with a gate and by giving a reward of 10 as an intermediate reward upon reaching the gate. Afterwards, if the agent achieves its goal an additional 90 points is given to get the same total of 100.

In this experiment, we use different sized mazes all having one wall. The target and agent locations are forced to be on different sides of the wall (this was not forced in previous experiments) and the intermediate reward area is given in a different color, close to white. We tested using different sizes of intermediate reward areas to check if extending the reward area increases the learning speed (see Fig. 8).

As we can see in Fig. 9, adding an intermediate reward increases the learning speed as the maze size gets larger. In the 8×8 setting, the search space is already so small that no intermediate reward seems necessary. But especially in the 16×16 maze with its larger search space it helps and is more helpful when the intermediate reward area gets larger.

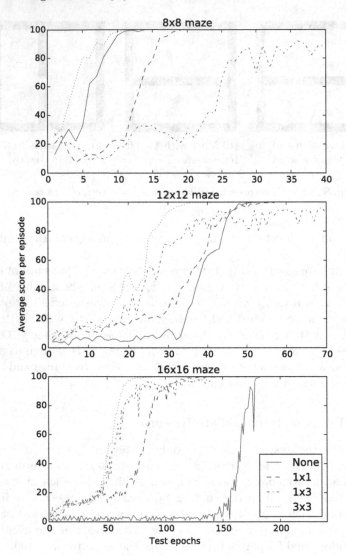

Fig. 9. Convergence of DQN as a function of maze size and the intermediate reward area. With small mazes intermediate reward does not help, but as the maze gets larger, larger areas of intermediate reward help more.

5 Pacman Experiments

For our next set of experiments, we use the game of Pacman, which is a more interesting maze game[2]. This environment provides customizable mazes and

---

[2] We use the Pacman environment prepared for the course UC Berkeley CS188 Introduction to AI, available at http://ai.berkeley.edu/reinforcement.html.

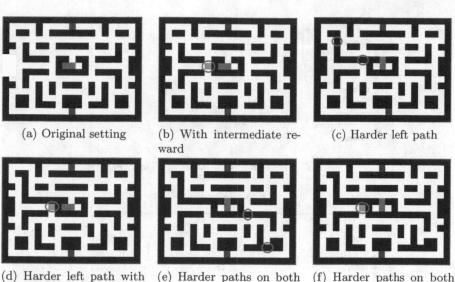

(a) Original setting

(b) With intermediate reward

(c) Harder left path

(d) Harder left path with intermediate reward

(e) Harder paths on both sides

(f) Harder paths on both sides with intermediate reward

(g) Harder left path with further intermediate reward

Fig. 10. The different setups of Ms. Pacman environment we tested DQN on. The agent starts from the bottom and tries to get the goal at the top. Two enemy units are shown at their spawn location in the center. Intermediate reward is colored in brighter gray. Changes between setups are denoted with red circles

basic AI options for enemy units. We adapted the maze style of the Ms. Pacman ATARI game to this environment and selected enemy units with random movement capabilities. These enemies pursue their path until they reach the end and select their next path randomly when they are at a junction point. A contact with an enemy ends the game with -500 reward points. Intermediate reward gives $+10$ points whereas the goal gives $+500$.

Just like in the maze experiments, we test for factors that change the complexity of the game to see their effect on the convergence of DQN. There are three factors: (a) There are two paths from the initial position at the bottom to the goal at the top, and one can block either of them or not, (b) There may be

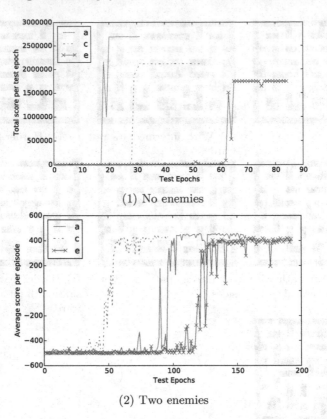

(1) No enemies

(2) Two enemies

Fig. 11. Comparison of DQN convergences on original Pacman setup (a), harder left path (c) and harder paths on both sides (e)

enemy units or not to avoid contact with, and (c) There may be intermediate rewards on the correct path. We also try combinations of those factors and in Fig. 10, we show the seven different setups. By training DQN in each of these setups with zero or two enemy units, we experiment with a total of fourteen different setups.

We start by closing some paths by adding obstacles (see Fig. 11). In setup (c), we make one of the two possible routes longer by closing some paths and in setup (e), both the leftmost and the rightmost solution paths are extended by adding obstacles. We can see in Fig. 11(1) that extending the leftmost path (c) decreases learning with respect to (a). However, if we examine Fig. 11(2), we can see that adding some enemy units to (c) increases the learning speed, since most of the time the agent gets destroyed in the leftmost path by the enemies, thus the agent learns that it should not dwell on the leftmost path concentrating on the correct path which is the rightmost path. If we compare setup (e) with (a) and (c), we see that making all possible paths longer decreases the learning speed, as expected.

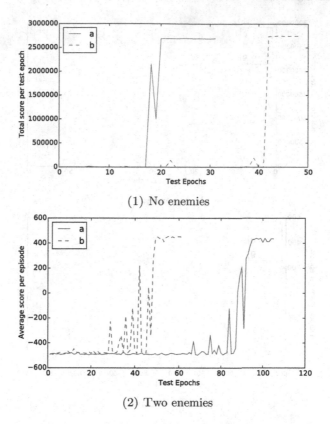

(1) No enemies

(2) Two enemies

Fig. 12. Comparison of DQN convergences on original Pacman setup (a) and intermediate reward (b)

If we examine setups (a) and (b) (see Fig. 12), we see that adding an intermediate reward increases DQN's learning speed considerably in the two-enemy setup. This is expected since the intermediate reward helps algorithm to focus on one of the two paths. In the no-enemy setup however, the agent learns getting the intermediate reward quickly, but it tends to stay near the intermediate reward for many epochs to come since ϵ value gets its lower bound in four epochs and the agent cannot explore the target quickly. Thus, it decreases the learning speed.

The intermediate reward in setup (d) was actually designed to hinder learning since it is en route to a longer path. In the no-enemy case, the results show that this reward actually hinders learning as can be seen in Fig. 13. After the agent takes this reward, instead of choosing the leftmost path, it uses the rightmost path which is the closer one to the target. However, it results with even better outcomes than setup (c) when there are enemies. The agent in this case is able to learn to choose between left or right paths according to the closeness of the enemies to those paths. In setup (g), we move the intermediate reward to a further position on the left path and saw that it decreases learning speed in

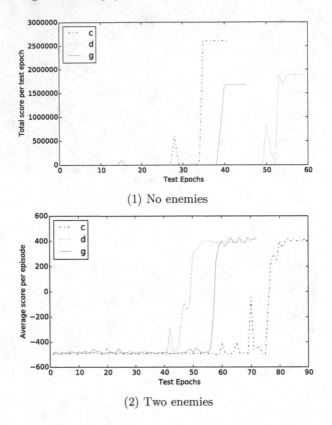

(1) No enemies

(2) Two enemies

Fig. 13. Comparison of DQN convergences on Pacman setup with harder left path (c), early intermediate reward (d) and hard intermediate reward (g)

no-enemy setup, better than (d). This also helps learning when there are two enemies and provides worse results than (d), because the risk of death is higher in the path with the intermediate reward. Nevertheless, when the algorithm converges, the agent is able to wait for risk of the opponents to pass and go back if it is necessary.

Comparison of setups (e) and (f) are given in Fig. 14. Similar to the previous results, since the ϵ value gets to its minimum value quickly, the intermediate reward in this case (f) slows down the learning process. Slow down rate is extremely high because most of the paths are blocked and the agent cannot get the target. It helps when there are enemies, because enemies force the agent to explore.

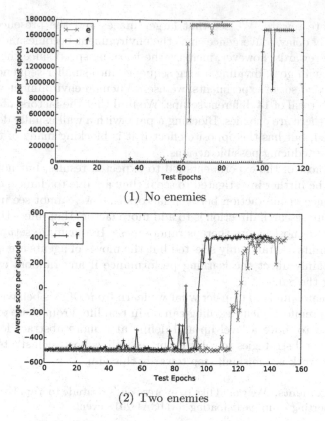

(1) No enemies

(2) Two enemies

Fig. 14. Comparison of DQN convergences on Pacman setup with harder paths on both sides (e) and intermediate reward (f)

6   Conclusions and Future Work

Deep reinforcement learning is a recent research area that combines deep neural networks with reinforcement learning. The Deep Q-Network learns to play Atari games end-to-end; but it learns some games better, some faster, and we do not know why. Our assumption is that the complexity of a game depends on some factors and these factors affect DQN's learning speed and quality.

To validate this claim, we clustered the DQN convergence curves of 45 ATARI 2600 games. We find that there seems to be indeed a dependence between game characteristics and DQN performance, that games that are played similarly are learned similarly by DQN and are placed nearby in the clustering dendrogram, whereas games that look the same visually but need different strategies are placed far apart.

We defined variants of a Maze task on which we defined a number of factors and tested their effect using DQN as it is, with no changes to the network architecture or learning algorithm. The four factors we tested are the maze size, presence/absence of walls, presence/absence of enemies, and presence/absence of intermediate reward. We see that larger mazes and the presence of enemy units generally delay convergence since the environment becomes more complex. Intermediate rewards, however, increase the learning speed since they provide a hint for the main goal, dividing a long sequence into smaller sequences.

In the second set of experiments, we use a Pacman environment with similar factors with a total of 14 different setups. We find that the factors affect learning differently if there are enemies. Blocking a path with a wall usually decreases the learning speed, but has the opposite effect if it is blocking many of the possible paths thereby reducing possible actions.

Overall, most of the experiments led to expected results, but not all. These cases should be further investigated to see if they are due to chance, or if there is any dependence or interaction between factors that we cannot see immediately. Another future research direction is to add more factors that affect the difficulty. For example, in most games there is randomness. In our maze setup, the initial positions of units are randomly selected but the moves of agents are not random; it could certainly affect the learning performance if any random event should occur during the game.

The ultimate aim is to transfer what we learn from DQN's behavior on games to what deep reinforcement learning can do in real life. From these experiments, we would like to move a level up and define at a more abstract level, general tasks and general strategies to solve them, as well as how such strategies can be learned. Our work is one small step towards this aim.

Acknowledgements. We would like to express our gratitude to Yapı Kredi Teknoloji A.Ş. for supporting us in participating to IJCAI 2018 events.

References

1. Anderson, D., Stephenson, M., Togelius, J., Salge, C., Levine, J., Renz, J.: Deceptive games. In: Sim, K., Kaufmann, P. (eds.) EvoApplications 2018. LNCS, vol. 10784, pp. 376–391. Springer, Cham (2018). https://doi.org/10.1007/978-3-319-77538-8_26
2. Bellemare, M.G., Dabney, W., Munos, R.: A distributional perspective on reinforcement learning. In: Proceedings of the 34th International Conference on Machine Learning-Volume 70, pp. 449–458. JMLR. org. (2017)
3. Berndt, D.J., Clifford, J.: Using dynamic time warping to find patterns in time series. In: Proceedings of the 3rd International Conference on Knowledge Discovery and Data Mining, AAAIWS 1994, pp. 359–370. AAAI Press (1994)
4. Elias, G.S., Garfield, R., Gutschera, K.R.: Characteristics of Games. The MIT Press, Cambridge (2012)
5. Hasselt, H.V., Guez, A., Silver, D.: Deep reinforcement learning with double q-learning. In: Proceedings of the Thirtieth AAAI Conference on Artificial Intelligence, AAAI 2016, pp. 2094–2100. AAAI Press (2016)
6. Hessel, M., Modayil, J., van Hasselt, H., et al.: Rainbow: combining improvements in deep reinforcement learning. In: Thirty-Second AAAI Conference on Artificial Intelligence (2018)

7. Levine, S., Finn, C., Darrell, T., et al.: End-to-end training of deep visuomotor policies. J. Mach. Learn. Res. **17**(39), 1–40 (2016)
8. Lillicrap, T.P., Hunt, J.J., Pritzel, A., et al.: Continuous control with deep reinforcement learning. ArXiv e-prints, September 2015
9. Mnih, V., Badia, A.P., Mirza, M., et al.: Asynchronous methods for deep reinforcement learning. In: Proceedings of the 33nd International Conference on Machine Learning, ICML 2016, New York City, NY, USA, 19–24 June 2016, pp. 1928–1937 (2016)
10. Mnih, V., Kavukcuoglu, K., Silver, D., et al.: Human-level control through deep reinforcement learning. Nature **518**(7540), 529–533 (2015)
11. Nair, A., Srinivasan, P., Blackwell, S., et al.: Massively parallel methods for deep reinforcement learning. ArXiv e-prints, July 2015
12. Peng, X.B., Berseth, G., van de Panne, M.: Terrain-adaptive locomotion skills using deep reinforcement learning. ACM Trans. Graph. **35**(4), 81:1–81:12 (2016). https://doi.org/10.1145/2897824.2925881
13. Schaul, T., Quan, J., Antonoglou, I., et al.: Prioritized experience replay. ArXiv e-prints, November 2015
14. Silver, D., Huang, A., Maddison, C.J., et al.: Mastering the game of go with deep neural networks and tree search. Nature **529**(7587), 484–489 (2016)
15. Silver, D., Hubert, T., Schrittwieser, J., et al.: Mastering Chess and Shogi by self-play with a general reinforcement learning algorithm. ArXiv e-prints, December 2017
16. Silver, D., Schrittwieser, J., Simonyan, K., et al.: Mastering the game of go without human knowledge. Nature **550**, 354–359 (2017)
17. Wang, Z., Schaul, T., Hessel, M., et al.: Dueling network architectures for deep reinforcement learning. In: Proceedings of the 33rd International Conference on International Conference on Machine Learning, ICML 2016, vol. 48, pp. 1995–2003. JMLR.org (2016)
18. Yannakakis, G.N., Togelius, J.: Artificial Intelligence and Games. Springer, Heidelberg (2018). http://gameaibook.org

Author Index

Printed in the United States
By Bookmasters